Characters In Search of a Novel

by

Molly D. Campbell

Illustrations by

Randy Palmer

Copyright © 2012 Molly D. Campbell

This book is a work of fiction. Names, characters, places and incidents are products of the author's imagination or are used fictitiously. Any resemblance to actual events or locales or persons, living or dead, is entirely coincidental.

All rights reserved. No part of this book may be reproduced or transmitted in any form or by any means, electronic or mechanical, including photocopying or recording, or by any information storage or retrieval system, without written permission of the author, except where permitted by law.

http://mollydcampbell.com
http://charactersinsearchofanovel.com

Illustrations and Front Cover Design by Randy Palmer
Cover and Text Design by A. Mitchkoski, D. Almstead, Writing Team
Managing Editor, Hazel Dawkins, The Writing Team

Library of Congress CIP Data: 1. Essays. 2. Whimsy. 3. Character sketches. Humor.

Campbell, Molly D.
Characters In Search of a Novel

This book is dedicated with much love to the members of my family—all of whom are characters.

Some Special Thank Yous

I would like to thank some people for helping me get to the point where a book was even possible. To Sheryl K., for informing me that I was a writer (really, I didn't realize it at the time). To Marion and Annie, for only rolling their eyes behind my back. To the Accordionist, for being a huge cheerleader between gigs. For Bryan, who showed me how to blog. To Beth Hoffman, who serves as inspiration on a daily basis. To Karen Black, who took time out from her successful writing career to tell me that Loretta Squirrels deserved more than a tweet. And to all of my wonderful Twitter writing friends, who have made my life at the desk in the pantry worth living. And to the Erma Bombeck Writers' Workshop, for allowing me to gain validation as a person who actually *can* write. Finally to my incredible team of experts: Randy Palmer, who I swear lives inside my head; Peter Pollock, who never met a challenge he didn't like; Hazel Dawkins, Aggie Mitchkoski, Derek Almstead, who don't miss a trick...*Can we all do this again?*

About the Illustrator

Randy Palmer was born in Dayton, Ohio, in 1957. After earning his Associate Degree in commercial art technology from Sinclair College, Randy was a technical inker and paste-up artist until the place he was working closed. On a whim, he called the Dayton (Ohio) *Daily News* Editorial Art Department, where he was offered a job coloring the weekend weather map. He has been with the newspaper since 1984. Randy's career highlights include an award of excellence from The Society of Illustrators, inclusion in the *Print Regional Design Annual* and a National Headliner Award. His work has appeared in numerous newspapers and magazines. Randy lives in Dayton with his wife, Jenny, and their daughters, Adrienne and Madeline.

Contents

Foreword by Ann Imig..	x
Dottie Mulcher	2
Loretta Squirrels...	6
Fingal Strafer...	10
Fred Smalls..	16
Alderton Potts...	20
Danny Violets..	24
Ardith Vellum..	28
Perry P..	32
Dinky Wells...	36
Daisy Norsuch...	40
Mavis Byway...	44
Lolly Luffington Barker..	48
Georgette Ambler...	52
Mrs. Mason..	56
The Tarnations..	60
Morty Portnoy..	64
Birdie Motts..	68
Patsy Purvis..	72
Little Randolph...	76
Annie Withers...	80
Judith Jones...	86
Marna Crosby...	90
Scarlet Swells..	94
Algernon..	98
Amos Cargill...	102
Mimsy Carrothers..	106
Sergeant Winteregg..	112
Wilma Trickles..	116
Veronica Stabbs..	120
Duke Devlin..	126
Marla Swaine..	130

The Cat Lady.. 134
Farley Spratt.. 138
The Maestro... 142
Florian Muenster... 146
Rachel Klenhauser... 150
Mom and Ida... 154
Hester Packmore.. 158
Horton Gooie... 164
Seth Jacobs... 168
Acantha Malwaring.. 172
Persis and Rex... 176
More Characters, Still Searching.................................... 181
About the Author... 183
Enthusiastic Reviews.. 189

Foreword

by Ann Imig

I met award-winning (PSYCHOPATH) humorist Molly D. Campbell on the Internet. Naturally, I soon found myself (AMBUSHED) across the country in a yurt with Molly in Ojai, California, at a conference for online (UNSUSPECTING VICTIMS) women. At that juncture, my Molly D. Campbell dossier included two facts: Her husband plays the accordion and they hail from the wilds of Dayton, Ohio. I listened yurt-side as Molly announced her plans to take over the blogosphere by hell or high-popularity, and as she proclaimed herself my number-one fan and (STALKER) surrogate Mother while trying to fit me in a Baby Bjorn.

In fact, I grew so enamored with Molly D. Campbell, that I promptly (WAS ABDUCTED) left my own family and moved into Molly and The Accordion Man's basement with nothing but my Famous Footwear Rewards card in my pocket and a sack of Dayton dreams tied to the end of a stick. I write this

Foreword (UNDER DURESS) while apprenticing Molly at her kitchen table, as we drink prune smoothies and she types on her beloved Commodore 64—our heads bobbing in time to *In Heaven There is No Beer*. The shackles hardly chafe at all any more, as my ankles now resemble Clydesdale hoofs—not having seen the likes of a razor in 18 months.

If you're familiar with Molly (RUN AWAY WHILE YOU STILL CAN), you already love the funny and poignant essays she deposits weekly on her blog *Life With The Campbells* from her Bombeck-ian brain. What none of us knew before *Characters In Search of a Novel*, however (I SAID RUN), was that an entire population of misfits hangs out in her cerebral cortex after Erma hours (WHEN SHE DEMANDS I SPOONFEED HER ONE CHOCOLATE RIESEN EVERY 3 MINUTES 7 SECONDS). Sometime between Happy Hour and Last Call, Molly entertains the likes of Loretta Squirrels, Dinky Wells, and Mavis Byway in her lymbic Casablanca. (RUN. YOU. FOOL.)

Herein lie the contents of this book—Molly's *Characters In Search of a Novel*. Or, perhaps a glimpse into the inner-workings of (THE WOMAN WHO WON'T STOP CALLING

ME BITSY) one of the most dynamic online characters of all—Molly D. Campbell herself (SEND HELP. FULLSTOP.)

*A stay-at-home humorist, Ann Imig has inflicted herself on your Internet since 2008 through her blog **annsrants.com** and various websites such as **collegehumor.com** and **McSweeneys Internet Tendency**. Ann founded and acts as national director for the nationwide live reading series LISTEN TO YOUR MOTHER. Learn more about her at **annimig.com**.*

Molly D. Campbell

The Characters

Characters In Search of a Novel

Dottie Mulcher

Her children adore her. As a matter of fact, *all* children adore her. My Lord, she's an Earth Mother! You know those fertility idols that are imported from Africa that they sell in posh gift catalogs? That is what Dottie looks like: big breasts, wide, childbearing hips, and low slung—just right for dropping the babies in the field and continuing to toil.

Dottie sets an example for the rest of us that we simply can't live up to. For instance, she makes these delicious molasses cookies with raisins in them that are to die for, and even though she has given all of us the recipe, none of us can make them to our children's satisfaction, so they just bring fistfuls home from Dottie's house.

Oh yes. Speaking of perfection: Dottie sews. Who does this, nowadays? She runs up Halloween costumes that are the wonder of the neighborhood. Last year, her twins were Tweedledee and Tweedledum, and I swear, they looked just like the ones in the Tim Burton movie! While I struggle filling garbage sacks with leaves and attaching a string and a label, praying my children will love the "teabag" idea, Dottie makes her daughter a "Big Bird" costume, complete with real yellow feathers.

Dottie's husband is really good looking. I know; it's catty of me, but really—how does a woman with big hips and peasant thighs attract a man with a six pack and silver hair? Is it those cookies, for Pete's sake? Ron Mulcher, despite his name, looks at home in a bomber jacket and moccasins with no socks. Dottie wears her nightgown to drive the kids to school, and I don't think she knows what mascara *is*. This is not fair.

I asked my husband if he thinks Dottie is attractive. And guess what? He said, "Well, she looks kind of edible." Good God. I go to Pilates three times a week, shave virtually every hair that isn't on my head, I dye my roots regularly, and look pretty good in jeggings, but Dottie is *edible*? I give up.

If I could, I would hate her. But here's another thing: Dottie is wonderful to everyone. She makes delish casseroles and brings them over whenever one of the kids gets strep, because "I know no one is getting much sleep over here." She grows beautiful roses, and distributes little bouquets around the neighborhood. For Christmas, we all get little bags of rosemary-roasted cashews. She buys full size Hershey bars and saves them to hand out to the kids in the neighborhood, rather than the "fun sized" ones she gives to all the other children. She never gossips.

I really don't know how she manages this. And did I mention that she has *buck teeth?*

Characters In Search of a Novel

Loretta Squirrels

She don't take nothin' from no one. Hell, she ain't had a Daddy her whole life, and her Mama left Loretta to take care of them babies most days. Loretta learnt how to shoot and how to cook what she kilt. Them babies never went hungry.

She don't take no shit. She don't have to, cause she's so big and mean. Loretta has to bend down to go through most doors, and I seen her kick a few in when they was locked! And if she gets drunk, git out of the way, cause Loretta gets to shoving folks around, then!

Loretta married Bobby Ray Squirrels when they was in eighth grade. She says she liked his eyes. Everyone says it's cause Bobby Ray had the best Moonshine recipe, and Loretta wanted that recipe more than anything else in the world. Moonshine is money in the bank. So now Bobby Ray and Loretta have a bidness. A real bidness. Loretta is the CEO. That means *Cheats Every One*.

Loretta don't never make mistakes. Hell, she says the only mistake she ever made was havin' too many babies. But Loretta raised 'em and kicked 'em out. Now she has all the time she needs to keep her stills goin' and keep Bobby Ray in line.

Loretta loves her music. She and Bobby Ray go over to Jesco's Grill on Friday nites, when they's got the bluegrass goin'. Hell, she sings right along with the band, and she gets louder and louder all nite! I seen her take her top off and shake around in her bra, but then Bobby Ray tole her to git her clothes on! Loretta can sing all nite long, and she never gets raspy or nothin'.

I hear that Loretta's cousin Harald tried to steal from Loretta's sister one time, and Loretta stabbed Harald for tryin'. I hear she used a fork. Man, that woman is mean! But shit, Harald should of knowed better. He was the one who showed Loretta how to use a gun, for cryin' out loud.

I used to be friends with her, but now I don't trust Loretta for shit. Hell, she came over my house and took four chickens! She says she did not, but I saw her runnin' off down the creek—she wrung their necks and shoved 'em in a poke! That Loretta oughta think about things. 'Fore she knows it, her and Bobby Ray won't have no more folks to depend on. What they call that? A support system? Well, she ain't gonna have one, no how, if she keeps stealin' poultry.

Characters In Search of a Novel

Fingal Strafer

This is an interview between "The New York Now" show and Mr. Fingal Strafer, successful prosecuting attorney at the prominent law firm, Strafer, Bangs, Stiffney and Shultz. Mr. Strafer has successfully prosecuted over one hundred cases without a single loss. (Cameras zoom in on the craggy Strafer, and Melanie Lusk, star reporter, wearing a sharkskin business suit and five-inch pumps.)

NYN: Mr. Strafer, how did you come to practice law, and why did you choose to become a prosecuting attorney?

FS: It's pretty straightforward, actually. I was the nerdy child of two rather scatterbrained artists, who dressed me in unusual clothing and sent me to public school, where I was bullied from the age of seven. I soon learned that a quick wit and good sneakers were my best defense. I hated those who dominated my world with violence, and vowed to do something about it when I grew up. So I have.

NYN: So you target bullies?

FS: I target those who assert power over others by putting them down. I have found that bullies usually grow up to do something unlawful during the pursuit of their power plays. I just make sure that they don't get away with it.

NYN: Do you ever come across female bullies?

FS: Of course. Women are just as fond of being in control of those weaker than they are as males. Women just use a different set of tools. Men commit crimes such as fraud, robbery, torture, and murder. Women do those things, but more often they are guilty of slander, sacrificing those who help them climb the success ladder, and ruining other people's marriages.

NYN: You sound a little bitter.

FS: I have been married four times. But only three of my wives were bitches. One died.

NYN: How do you prepare for a tough case?

FS: I stay in shape physically. I like to run, and I generally do around thirty miles a week. I don't drink while on a case, and I keep my mind sharp by studying codes and encryption. I love to write in code, and to code-break. Let's just say I don't like secrets.

NYN: (Clears throat) That is an interesting hobby. Do you have any other interests outside of those? What do you do for fun?

FS: I have sex with women. Other than that, I can't think of anything. Well, I do enjoy chess.

NYN: (Gulps) Ok then. (Shifts in her seat, and uncrosses her legs) What was your most difficult case?

FS: About ten years ago, we prosecuted a man for running a Ponzi scheme. He had convinced a group of retired people that if they gave him their money, he would make sure that they had visitors every day at their nursing homes. At first, it was wonderful, but then the old people started dying. Their families, who up to this time had felt relieved that their aging parents had stopped calling them, discovered that entire estates had been engulfed and disappeared, and the shit hit the fan. We sent the guy to prison for twenty years. I tried to stipulate that he get no visitors, but failed. (He smirks)

NYN: (Leaning backwards just a bit in her seat) Interesting. Are you working on anything right now that you can share with us?

FS: I am not able to say much. But it will make headlines. I can only say that if you have a dog, and you use a dog walking service, you should be careful.

NYN: I see. (Raises eyebrows at camera two)

FS: Dogs are disappearing. That's all I can say.

NYN: Goodness. Well, what a relief to know that you are working on this! Thank you for talking with us today. (Shuffles the papers in her lap)

FS: Do you have a dog?

NYN: (Shifts in chair uncomfortably, and adjusts skirt) Again, thanks. We will be looking forward to hearing about your next case, and I congratulate you on your fine work.

FS: I used to have a dog but he died. (Sniffs audibly and leans forward, brushing against Melanie's thigh with his hand) I love dogs. Just love dogs. (Sighs dramatically).

NYN: That's a shame. (Blinks rapidly) And now, we go to London, where Dan Strank is reporting live about the latest financial crisis.

FS: Yeah, my dog's name was "Slinky." (Sniffs again, and wipes one eye)

NYN: (Whispering urgently) *Cut, and that's a wrap!*

FS: (As production assistants lead him out) He had a little red bone....

Characters In Search of a Novel

Fred Smalls

Today in class, Mrs. Wellman gave us a stupid assignment. We have to describe our favorite person and what he/she means to us. I am fifteen, and for miles around, I have not one single favorite person. My parents are annoying know-it-alls, my sisters are pains in the butt, and all the girls in school are either chasing boys and forming cliques or picking their faces.

I do have one very favorite, however. My dog Fred is amazing. So I am going to do the assignment all right. I am going to describe my best friend Fred Smalls (by the way, my name is Starla Smalls—didn't I say that my parents are annoying?)

<u>My Best Friend, Fred Smalls</u>

By Starla Smalls, English 2, Mrs. Wellman, Fourth period

Fred Smalls is a very energetic, small man with short brown and white hair. That is, the hair on the top of his head is brown, and it fades to white around his ears. Fred has kind of droopy ear lobes. Fred's eyes are small and brown. His teeth were pretty good looking until he turned ten, when they started to get a little yellow, but most people think that Fred Smalls is quite attractive.

Fred Smalls is a bachelor. He came to live with my family as a very young boy, and my parents adopted him. My parents are very controlling people, and they never let Fred go out on any dates or get married. I think they might have even considered some sort of medical intervention at one point, but Fred Smalls still has balls.

Fred Smalls is unemployed. He spends most of his time hanging around the house with my mother, and he is very fond of me. When I come home from school, Fred sits at the desk with me and assists me with word problems and Latin declensions. After that, Fred often suggests that we take a walk or play some ball, just to take the edge off things for me. Fred understands that ninth grade is very stressful, especially for girls who don't belong to the right cliques. Fred also encourages me not to pick my face, which helps a lot.

Fred is a nudist. Since he spends most of his time in the privacy of our home, this is appropriate. Fred, thanks to my mother, has few friends, but all of them are nudists as well.

Fred does wear an occasional red or blue bandanna, and some of his friends are apparently into S and M, because a couple of them, Bud and Thunder, wear those leather-studded necklaces.

Fred has an extensive vocabulary, and he also has very expressive eyes. He tells me when he is happy, sad, hungry, itchy, and when he has to go to the bathroom. I guess you could call Fred a bit slow, but I have known some straight A students that seem dumber than Fred Smalls.

Fred is a happy man. I think he feels satisfied with his accomplishments in life. He owns his own one-bedroom house, he has a close family, he has a huge arsenal of toys, including some that squeak, and he lives very well without having a career. Fred has learned the secret of happiness in life. All you need is a loving family, some great nudist friends, moderate exercise, and beef jerky.

Characters In Search of a Novel

Alderton Potts

When he was little, he went out of his way not to step on any bugs. Puppies followed him home. His mother promised him that she wouldn't set any mousetraps, so she did it after Aldy went to bed, and got up early to hide the carnage.

Aldy Potts also loved his fellow humans. When he was seven, he saved a little girl who was wading into the pond after some very attractive ducklings. She would have drowned, but Aldy prevailed. The little girl's mother had Aldy over for tea, and afterwards drew him to her bosom in a rather smothering hug.

When he was almost eighteen, Aldy was in London, visiting his Great Aunt Hattie Potts. They were walking down a shady lane, and a lurker began to follow them. The ruffian jostled into Aunt Hattie, in an obvious ploy to steal her pocketbook. In it was their train fare home, as well as a few shillings extra. Aunt Hattie, being of slender means, was shocked and horrified. In her terror, she relinquished her beaded bag.

Aldy was not going to have it, not at all! He rushed after the miscreant, and with one mighty blow, sent the man to the cobbles. He regained his Aunt's accessory, and just before the man ran off, Alderton fixed him with a fearful gaze and cried, "You had better mend your ways, you scofflaw!" Then Aldy escorted Aunt Hattie to the nearest constabulary to report the crime.

That was just the beginning. My stars. Aldy stopped a hold-up on a bus. He saved an innocent from a devious predator. His neighbors invoked his name whenever they were in danger, or even just a little scared.

It dawned on him during his twentieth birthday celebration, when he overturned a burglary in progress on the lawn: despite his plus fours and Scally cap, Alderton Potts was a superhero.

Molly D. Campbell

Characters In Search of a Novel

DANNY VIOLETS

He wears one of those little "hipster" hats. He's never without shades. He has perfected a cocky swagger. I see him going in and out of the convenience store across the street, and he hangs around with some pretty shady looking guys. He's got bandy legs and buggy eyes. He's a crook.

But Danny would rather be a film critic. He loves movies. He goes to three or four a week. He can recite the dialogue from every "Godfather" movie from memory. He thinks that Harry Potter sucks. Danny loves the smell of popcorn, a big box of Good and Plenty, and those sticky theater floors. Danny lives for flicks.

He remembers the first time he entered a theater. He was with his older sister, Margaret, and his Aunt Flora. Flora had taken pity on her sister Dora, and told her that she would take the kids to the movies so Dora could get a rest. Danny and Margaret were wild ones.

Danny didn't know what to expect, but as soon as he entered the lobby with its red velvet ropes, flocked gold wallpaper, and delicious scent of popcorn, he felt transported. Flora bought them each a box of popcorn and some licorice to share. Danny felt like a king. As they settled into their burgundy "velvet" seats, Danny's feet felt the sticky floor, tacky from years of spilt soft drinks. He loved the wooden armrests with their patina of age.

First there was a cartoon about a stupid cat and smart mice. Danny and Margaret thought it was hilarious. The theater filled with the hoots and chortles of both children and adults alike, and Danny thrilled at the feeling of shared laughter and the excitement of what was to come.

There were previews of coming attractions. A cowboy movie with showdowns and a battle with Indians. Danny wanted to know how that one ended, and whispered loudly to Aunt Flora, "Will you bring us to see that one, too?" Flora shushed him loudly, and so Danny held his tongue.

The feature film was by someone called Walt Disney. It was about a little fawn whose mother died, killed by hunters. Danny and Margaret sobbed throughout. Margaret went on to name her first daughter "Bambi." Danny vowed never to shoot anyone or anything with a gun. He was later to renege on that promise to himself.

Danny never married, but he has two kids with his girlfriend, Carmen. He takes them to the movies as often as he can. They like things that are full of violence and action. Maybe it's because that is the life they are used to. But Danny is a good father in his own way, and they always get popcorn and licorice, and sometimes they watch the same movie more than once.

I just got off the phone. It was my mother's neighbor, Dora Violets. She was crying and howling. It seems that just last week, Danny took his kids to the Saturday matinee. They had lots of fun rooting for the aliens against the humans. It was a spectacular movie.

On the way home, Danny got into a scuffle with some goons from the other side of town, and before you could say "Mission Impossible," Danny had a bullet hole in his chest. The kids were not harmed, thank goodness. But Danny may be laid up for awhile.

Dora wanted to know if I had the "Godfather" DVD set.

Characters In Search of a Novel

Ardith Vellum

She sees things that nobody else does. Most people just *look* at things, and they really don't *see*. There are a very few individuals walking the earth that can tell us what is really there. Ardith is one of them.

She writes about pain, and beauty, and love. Then when the rest of us read what she writes, we can feel the love and the pain the way she does. And we are better people. That is what poetry is for. Of course, this is just my opinion. But there are lots of folks out there who find something like truth in Ardith's writing, because she is now selling her work to readers in far-flung places like France, Italy, Africa, and Sweden. People are paid to try to translate her poems so that they sound as much like Ardith's own words as possible. I am assured that they are good at this, but I really don't see how this could possibly work. To me, you have to imagine Ardith reciting her poems in her gentle voice to appreciate them.

Ardith is a very small person, but she is filled with huge things inside. You can see it in her eyes. They are greenish brown, and so enormous that they seem to fill her face. The first time I saw Ardith, I was so riveted by her eyes that I didn't even notice how her hair gleamed, or that her complexion was perfect. With Ardith, it is all in the eyes.

Ardith carries a little notebook in her purse at all times. She jots down little phrases and colorful descriptions of things: "For future reference," she says. Then when she gets home, she transcribes all of the things she has written down that day into a large journal. I think she must have hundreds of them. Then, when "inspiration vibrates," she says, she just opens her journals, leafs through them, and starts to write. She writes on beautiful, thick paper that costs quite a bit of money, but according to Ardith, it is "essential to my existence as an artist." So I buy it for her in huge boxes. It's the only thing that she requires. Ardith shuns fashion and jewelry. She has pared life down to just the things that she really needs. As a matter of fact, I don't think I have ever heard Ardith say that she "wanted" anything, really.

I watch her. She writes by hand. Ardith says that a keyboard is just too clinical. The keys "put her off." So she sits at her small desk in front of the window, and she writes. She prefers to write at sunset, or "in the gloaming," but sunsets are so fleeting—she often stays rooted to the spot for hours, the words pouring out of her.

She lets me read what she writes, because she says that she thinks it would break my heart if she didn't. She is right. I would love to understand the workings behind those eyes of hers, and reading her words opens me up somehow. I can't explain this, because I am too "prosaic," according to Ardith. My favorites are the little verses that she writes for babies. These are musical and full of color. She doesn't write too many of those any more. Some of her poems are full of desolation. When I read those, I feel helpless.

Some people worry about Ardith. I worry, too. She is so small, after all. And her eyes seem a little duller. Now when she sits at her desk, she doesn't even look out the window. Sunsets or not. But I still watch her. I guess you could say that these days, I watch *over* her. I just want to make sure that she is all right, and that her words don't overwhelm her. I try to be encouraging and cheerful.

I tell her that we can still have children.

Characters In Search of a Novel

Perry P

Dear Diary,

Today I bought the most glorious boa: pink feathers with sequins! Divine! It will look flashy with the jeggings and patent boots. Rudy is mad with envy, but I told him that if he wants to work his jazzy butt off like I do, then maybe he can do a little more shopping. My God. He just stays in bed all day, watching Oprah and Ellen, giving me orders. Someday I will just sashay right out of here!

Oh, and I have a secret. Don't tell a soul! But I met the most gorgeous man today! He walked into the store, and asked me for help with pajamas. He bought three silk sets, and insisted on trying them all on "for size." He asked me for special help in the fitting room. It was heaven, I tell you!

Mama called. She keeps asking me when I am going to get married. I told her that as soon as I can get Rudy out of bed, we are going to go right down to the city offices and make it legal, now that New York has seen the light. Mama doesn't believe it. She says that Rudy is too selfish to be a good husband. But what does she know about husbands, anyway? She's never had one herself, and all her men have been drunks. At least Rudy knows when he's had too many Cosmopolitans.

I went to the doctor yesterday. The electrolysis is going well. It only stings a little. She says that after another four visits, my beard will be gone completely. As soon as I save up, I am going to have her do my chest. Divine!

On a sad note, Evan's pit bull, Liza, died last week. She had been having some kind of fits, and the medicine just didn't work. Evan was beside himself, and even when the boys all came over and opened champagne, it didn't help. We all pitched in to buy the most cunning little urn for Liza's ashes. Pink and green enamel with gold leaf. Not real gold, but still quite stunning. I think he appreciated it, but the tears just won't stop flowing.

After the funeral, Rudy got on PetFinder and started searching for Malti-Poos. I told him that if we are going to have a pet, he should consider a cat. We have been over all this before: doggies need to pee! And who is going to have to take it out to do that? **Rudy.** I am working! Rudy never listens. I am more than delighted to change a cat box, and a cat would be so entertaining! Malti-Poos. Who does Rudy think is going to keep all that white hair fluffy? And who will take it to the groomers? I certainly won't. Rudy is just spoiled.

I want a parrot.

Characters In Search of a Novel

Dinky Wells

She's a squealer. It doesn't matter what: Dinky squeals when she sees a puppy, when it thunders, if the doorbell rings, or when cookies come out of the oven. Dinky is full of energy. She moves really fast for a pudgy person, and she never seems to get tired.

Dinky Wells writes songs. She wanted to be a famous country singer, but she had to face the fact that her singing was squealy, too, and so now she *writes* songs. Most of them are about either love gone wrong or truckers. I told her that all country songs are about love gone wrong or truckers, and she has to start writing about something more original, like farmers or pole dancers, but she just told me to shut up.

Dinky has a heart of gold, though. She has personally saved five dogs and a whole lot of kittens. She just sees them on the highway, stops her car, and takes them to the vet. I have asked around, and nobody else I know has *ever* spied a kitten running along the highway. I call her the "stray magnet." Dinky finds homes for all these critters, too.

One song that Dinky wrote I did like. It was about one of those ice road truckers. You know the ones on that show, who drive all that equipment up to Alaska or somewhere, and it's very dangerous? Well, Dinky's song was about one of them, and he had a broken heart and a broken axle at the same time. It was terribly sad. He nearly died out there in the blizzard, replacing that axle. So maybe Dinky will get famous after all.

Dinky and my cousin used to go out. I thought maybe they'd get married, but Dinky threw Randy over for another guy. Randy took it hard, and for a while he drank too much. Dinky felt bad about it, but what with the new boyfriend, saving dogs and writing songs, she just got on with her life. Randy hasn't been the same since, and he has gotten fat and has pimples now. It's so sad.

Dinky says that she will probably never get married. She says men take the wind out of your sails. I guess she just can't justify all the attention that a husband would want. Dinky likes the wifely things enough, but she just has too many other things to do. Maybe someday, she says. After she gets famous. Then she might get a wedding ring.

I like Dinky a lot. She sure has her goals set up. And she just eats life right up, what with all the squealing and the dogs and kittens. And the songs. She's kind of like a role model for me.

I can sing, though.

Characters In Search of a Novel

Daisy Norsuch

She always wanted to be a mother. Her favorite books growing up involved busy families, precocious children, and wonderful, old houses. She had names for her children chosen from her favorite books in the ready, long before she got married: Anne, from *Anne of Green Gables*, Amy, from *Little Women*, and Charlotte, after Charlotte Bronte. She did not plan to have any boys.

Daisy married her high school sweetheart, Ian Norsuch. Ian worked very hard teaching Modern Languages at the local university. Daisy bought antiques. Soon, they had a rambling house and twin boys. So much for Daisy's plans! Charlie and Hank were followed a few years later by Anne, and when Holly (Daisy also loved Capote) was born as a little "surprise" when Anne was five, the family was complete.

Daisy now lives in a continual frenzy. She would not have predicted that her life would turn out this way! In a typical day, Daisy must: referee at least one fight, entice a stubborn toddler to eat their cereal, wash two loads of laundry, attempt to remember to shave her legs in the shower, chauffeur her own and others' kids to music lessons, walk the dog, vacuum something, and make dinner.

Just yesterday, little Holly asked her mother where babies come from. Daisy, who was driving the car, trying to find the "Barney" CD, craving chocolate, and not really listening, replied "Oh, honey, I think they get them from a catalog."

Daisy is not really overweight. But she is just so very rushed that she doesn't have time to exercise, other than to chase children. So the Girl Scout Cookies and graham crackers have gravitated to her hips. She has every intention of enrolling in some sort of fitness class, as soon as all of her children start school. So she wears Spanx under her jeans and hopes that her underarms won't start jiggling the way her mother's do.

Daisy has a degree in Computer Programming. She has considered using her computer skills to start a blog, and so far she has come up with a blog title: "The Feverish Feminist." Not that she is one, but she just loves the title. She has yet to do one post, because the children are on the computer a lot playing games, Ian has his fantasy teams on it, and during the day, Daisy is just too busy.

So when the phone rang, and the caller was from the local historical society, asking if the Norsuches would be willing to be included in the local "historical homes" tour, Daisy wasn't really listening. She thought the woman was asking Daisy if her home was historical, and Daisy absently answered, "Yes."

So now Daisy has exactly three weeks to turn her haphazard, cluttered, pudding-splattered house into a showplace. Ian leaves for Belgium on a student-exchange visit the day after tomorrow. Anne is in a play at school, and the twins sound as if they are getting tonsilly. The cable is out, and Daisy's neighbor is sending her children over for playgroup on the next two Mondays. Daisy is considering going *underground*.

Characters In Search of a Novel

Mavis Byway

She has her own office. It is small, but very neatly arranged. Every day, there is a fresh little flower in a bud vase on her desk. She hates bulletin boards, so she made a tasteful flowered pin-up board for important notices. There is a basket for stray papers, and not one dust mote in the air.

Mavis is a proofreader. She knows every grammar rule by heart. When in grade school, Mavis learned to diagram sentences, and ever after, Mavis loved the orderliness of the English language. Dangling participles be damned! Subjects and predicates *must* agree. But for Mavis, the worst sin of all is this newfangled concept that it is acceptable to call a single person "they." Whoever came up with *that* practice is a criminal, as far as she is concerned.

Mavis is orderly in all things. Her lunch is neatly packed every day. Every day, the same lunch: a cheese sandwich on white bread, no crusts, with a touch of mayonnaise. One Golden Delicious apple. One butter cookie. Mavis drinks water; coffee is way too stimulating. She eats at her desk; it saves time.

Mavis reads copy for both of her town newspapers. She has eyes like a hawk, and nothing escapes her notice. Two years ago, the editor wondered out loud if using "spell check" wouldn't be more efficient than paying a full-time proofreader, but Mavis and her zealous accuracy prevailed.

Red is her favorite color. Since it is so bright, Mavis only allows herself little "touches" of it here and there. She has one red sweater, a nice red wallet, and one plaid scarf with a red border. She once considered buying a red car, but felt that might be just a little too showy. Instead, she bought a three-year-old blue Chevrolet with good mileage.

Mavis lives in a small apartment. It is her haven. She spent years perfecting the atmosphere. The kitchen has a wonderful collection of copper pots that Mavis acquired one by one at estate sales. Her laminate countertops gleam: vintage Formica. She has a tea caddy from Fortnum and Mason, a souvenir from her one trip to London. Her living room is cozy. There is no fireplace, but Mavis let her love of red run riot on the walls, and so the room is always warm. She bought a worn-out Turkish rug at a garage sale, and it really sets off her furniture. She favors antiques, but on her salary, she scouts faithful reproductions. She loves books and collects miniatures.

Mavis has chronic shingles.

Characters In Search of a Novel

Lolly Luffington Barker

Lolly isn't delicate. It seems that she was born big: her mother, Sally, named her big baby "Lolita," having just seen the movie by that name, and hoping for some of that loveliness to rub off on her not-so-little one. Lolly grew up with lots of good food but few friends.

When she was sixteen, Lolly fell in love. With dogs. She witnessed a stray being kicked by some young hoodlums, and she made sure those boys learned their lesson! She took the unfortunate home, named him Marbles, and taught him how to jump through hoops. They were inseparable.

Marbles died when Lolly was twenty-five. By then, he was old and tired. He did his last few tricks with reluctance and then just laid down to rest. Lolly, although heartbroken, knew it was for the best. After he died, Lotty was heavy-hearted for just a little while, and then she realized that there must be more dogs where Marbles came from.

She started looking for strays, and my goodness, she saw them on almost every street corner. Before long, Lolly's modest home was full of seven dogs, one or two expecting puppies. She began to worry. Money was scarce. Lolly had a job, but working on a loading dock didn't pay much.

She asked her Pastor, Reverend Flitch, what she should do. He told her to "seek and she would find." Lolly, big of heart and body but not of mind, took this literally. She began to steal. Just enough to pay for dog food and wormer. Nothing else. She took a bit from the overflowing collection plate—after all, it was Pastor Flitch who told her in the first place. There was a tip on the table at the coffee shop when she sat down, so she took it. Her sister's purse always had a few extra dollars in it.

So Lolly and her dogs prevailed. By the time Lolly was thirty, she had fourteen dogs. Her back yard had no grass, just trampled down dirt. The house was clean, though, and every dog had a nice bed, decent food, and a polite way with strangers. There was little barking; Lolly held firm on *that*. And no one she stole from seemed to notice.

When she was approaching forty, her favorite dog, Beano, got sick. Lolly panicked, loaded him into her truck, and took him twenty miles to the emergency dog doctor. Miles Barker, D.V.M., didn't look too much like a doctor. He stood six feet six, weighed close to three hundred pounds, and had a lazy eye. It turned out that Beano had swallowed a rock! Dr. Miles did an emergency surgery that saved Beano's life. Lolly couldn't pay the bill, so she filched some cash from the donation jar on the counter.

I heard that Lolly and Dr. Miles got married. She answers the phones at his office, and they take in strays. Lolly gives them all names. She and Miles make good money, and Lolly puts a huge donation in the collection plate every Sunday. Her sister keeps finding money in odd corners of her house. And Lolly is a *big* tipper. I hear she is very happy, and that her twins are big-boned.

Characters In Search of a Novel

GEORGETTE AMBLER

Life is rough in college. So many eight o'clock classes. My God, and now that weekends start on Wednesday nights, it gets harder and harder to make even the classes that start after noon. Me and Georgette just keep getting further and further behind.

Georgette's parents had high hopes for her when they sent her off to this college. So did mine, but I think they have a firmer grip on reality than Georgette's. For instance, when my parents brought me up here, they only allowed me to take my laptop and a toaster oven. Georgette's parents brought up her entire wardrobe, which included seventeen pairs of shoes. They also toted up her "fun size" refrigerator and a microwave oven, an iron and ironing board, and two cocktail dresses. And this college is *above* the Mason-Dixon line.

So the fact that we both smoke (tobacco and some other plants), drink brown drinks, and eat processed American Cheese food would probably distress the Amblers. All my parents' hope for is passing grades and a B.A. degree in less than seven years. So it's a little harder for Georgette to maintain the façade.

There was a party last weekend, and I think we spent the night at the apartment of some guy named Darius or Darnell. Or maybe it was Josh. There were a few closet orgies, and the last thing I remember is Georgette dancing on the beer pong table. We woke up the next day with massive forehead crushers, and Georgette couldn't find her underwear.

At midterms, I managed to pull out a C in Bio Chem, but I failed Women's Studies. Can you believe that? But I just couldn't get through those books by Bella Abzug and Betty Friedan. They seemed so unattractive. Could they have even *gotten* dates?

Anyway, we struggled through our freshman year, and I ran out of money towards the end. I got a part time job at the Mini Mart just off campus. I sold beer to some suspiciously underage-looking boys, drank an incredible amount of coffee, learned how to operate the hot dog roasting rotisserie machine (delish), and sold two winning lottery tickets. It wasn't too bad.

During finals week, Georgette and I tried to cram, and we didn't see too much of each other. Finals were brutal. There was only *one party* that week. After finals, everybody was in a rush, packing up their shit and waiting for their parents to drive to campus to pick them up. I hardly saw Georgette.

But on the day the dorms closed, she came into the store, gave me a hug, and then looked around for a while. Then she came up to the counter.

She bought a bottle of Yoo-hoo and a pregnancy test.

Characters In Search of a Novel

Mrs. Mason

Every precocious little girl should have an old lady for a friend. Adults are much more interesting than children. Adults know about the world. Adults know great big words, and use them without affectation. For a child who is easily bored with childish things, an older woman can be the friend that changes life forever.

My lady friend was named Mrs. Mason. She lived next door with her irascible husband Kermit, their two adultish children, and lots and lots of books. Mrs. Mason (I was absolutely *not* allowed to call her Rebecca) had a college education, a charming lack of commitment to keeping house, and a real *library*. In our house, that room was called a "rec" room, and it had our TV in it. At the Masons, the television was in the living room, and the big room on the first floor was full of books.

I went over to the Masons' house just about every day after school. I was always welcome. I followed Mrs. Mason around, watching her make supper, plant seeds, or we just sat and talked. We talked about adult things, like politics and the neighbors. I gave my opinion, and she listened. Mrs. Mason was a terrible cook, and so when she wanted to make something good, she always asked for my help. We would make a treat, and go downstairs to the library while we waited for it to bake. Mrs. Mason would bring the laundry into the library and do some ironing, while I browsed through the books, looking for a good one. I could borrow any book I wanted to. Some of the books I read from Mrs. Mason's library included *The Thirteen Clocks*, which scared the daylights out of me; *The Complete Works of Rabelais*, which luckily had some illustrations that gave a rough idea of the goings on; and *Wuthering Heights*, which Mrs. Mason and I both **loved**, and which we discussed at length.

I was an eccentric child, and revelled in my friendship with the Mason family. None of them minded my constant presence, and all gave me the respect that most adults reserve for each other and rarely grant to kids. Apparently, the Masons were also eccentrics, but I didn't realize that. I thought all next-door neighbors dried their own herbs, dabbled in oil painting, let all the dishes sit in the sink to wash "tomorrow," and listened to classical music on the stereo full blast.

My mother worried that I was an annoyance next door, and she tried her best to interest me in more age-appropriate pursuits, like the Girl Scouts, roller skating, and dancing lessons, but I remained steadfastly devoted to Mrs. Mason. Finally, my mother gave up, and Mrs. Mason and I continued being best chums. We experimented in making our own ink out of flowers, which didn't work. We grew cactuses. We painted faces on rocks and placed them artfully in the garden. But more than anything, we talked about books.

When I went to high school, I saw less and less of Mrs. Mason, who seemed very understanding. We were still very friendly, but I just ran out of spare time. However, until I got married and moved away, I made the trip next door once in awhile.

I am now at about the same age that Mrs. Mason was when we met. I don't have a "library" in my house, but I wish I did. I am a bit eccentric. I actually *have* dried some herbs successfully. I sometimes let the dishes sit in the sink for a while.

But I don't have a seven-year-old best friend.

Characters In Search of a Novel

The Tarnations

When Mildred Hanbath married Arthur Tarnation, it was the beginning of a dynasty. Mildred was a very interesting woman, and Arthur had his quirks. Their children inherited both.

First born was a strapping boy with flailing fists and big lungs. His hearty crying could be heard by all the neighbors. Named Hugh, but called Big Hughie, he used his loud voice and powerful build to bully his classmates and win football games. The day Hughie spied Eleanor Rumpert coming down the hall, his knees went weak. It took a bold girl like Eleanor to calm Hughie down. Thanks to Eleanor, Hughie learned to use his inside voice and to put his napkin on his lap, where it belonged. Eleanor taught Hughie how to cook, and Hughie often donned an apron and made fudge.

Hughie's sister, Tallie Tarnation, was not quite as bold as her brother, and she certainly didn't match him in voice. Tallie was a whisperer. It seemed to her that the whole world rang out with clanging noises, and she got headaches. It soothed her to hear her little voice, and she spoke softly to herself for comfort. Tallie hated her alliterative name, but was too shy to do anything about it like getting married, so she stayed at home with Arthur and Mildred, tending to their needs, hushing them when possible, and keeping to herself when she could. But Tallie had birds. Her canaries sang beautifully, and they were just loud enough to be cheering. Tallie named them Custard and Fleece.

When Big Hughie and Eleanor got married, they moved just around the corner from their parents. Every Thursday evening, the Tarnations got together for supper. Mildred made pot roast with creamed potatoes, and Hughie brought fudge. Eleanor brought a cake, and Tallie made tea and lemonade. Hughie and Tallie did the dishes, so that Eleanor could watch the good TV shows with the elder Tarnations. Custard and Fleece were allowed to fly freely, and often landed on the television. Arthur laughed very loudly.

Hughie and Eleanor had a bit of trouble starting a family, but once started, they found it hard to stop. First came baby Bertha, followed very quickly by a set of twins: Ray and Randolph. After that, Eleanor thought she was finished, but five years later Gwendolyn was born. Gwen was a real firecracker, and after she nearly burned the garage down playing "campfire," Eleanor had a procedure done. And thank goodness for Tallie, who stayed with the children when Eleanor needed a breather. And even after Gwen pulled out Custard's tail feathers, Tallie remained a steadfast nanny.

The years went by. Bertha learned calligraphy. Ray and Randolph went away to college. Gwen threw pottery. Tallie continued whispering her support.

Life ran smoothly for the Tarnations. Then Eleanor entered menopause, and everything changed.

Characters In Search of a Novel

Morty Portnoy

Here's the thing. Morty Portnoy is Catholic. He goes to mass and everything. But it doesn't matter. Nobody believes it when he tells them. This is a curse on Morty, who in turn curses his parents, who apparently thought that having a problematic name builds character. Kind of like that boy named "Sue."

There is some mixture in the bloodlines; Morty is sure of *that*. Because with a mother whose maiden name was Sophie Elana O'Reilly and a father named Blanchard Portnoy, there had to be a whole ethnic cauldron bubbling up in that family. So he can't truly hold a huge grudge against his parents. But he *has* asked them repeatedly why they chose *Morton* for a first name, and *Robert* as a middle name. Couldn't they have switched? It seems to Morty that this was a cruel thing to do. But his mother just gives the same reply: "Would you rather we chose 'Horton' for your middle name?" Yeah, "Morton Horton Portnoy" would have been worse. She has him there.

Morty has considered changing his name to something a little more Catholic. Like Liam. But "Liam Portnoy" just doesn't seem to fit. Morty is a Morty, through and through. For instance, would somebody named "Liam" have wire-rimmed glasses? Would a "Liam" be a hypochondriac? And would somebody named "Liam Portnoy" play the organ and sing in the choir? So then Morty thought that perhaps he could just finesse his *last* name just a little. Portney? It was great, until he put his first name in front of it, and got "Morty Portney." No. Porter? "Morty Porter." Naw.

Morty asked around, and the consensus was just to grin and bear it. Take communion. Have a pastrami sandwich. Say a few Hail Mary's and call it a day.

But then Morty fell in love. With the most beautiful girl in the world. Smart, generous, tolerant and, luckily, with a good sense of humor. After about a year, they got engaged. It will be a big wedding, with both sides of the family equally represented. They can't decide on a venue. But they think that a non-denominational wedding might be best.

Next June, Morty Portnoy will wed the lovely Fatimah Horvath.

Molly D. Campbell

Characters In Search of a Novel

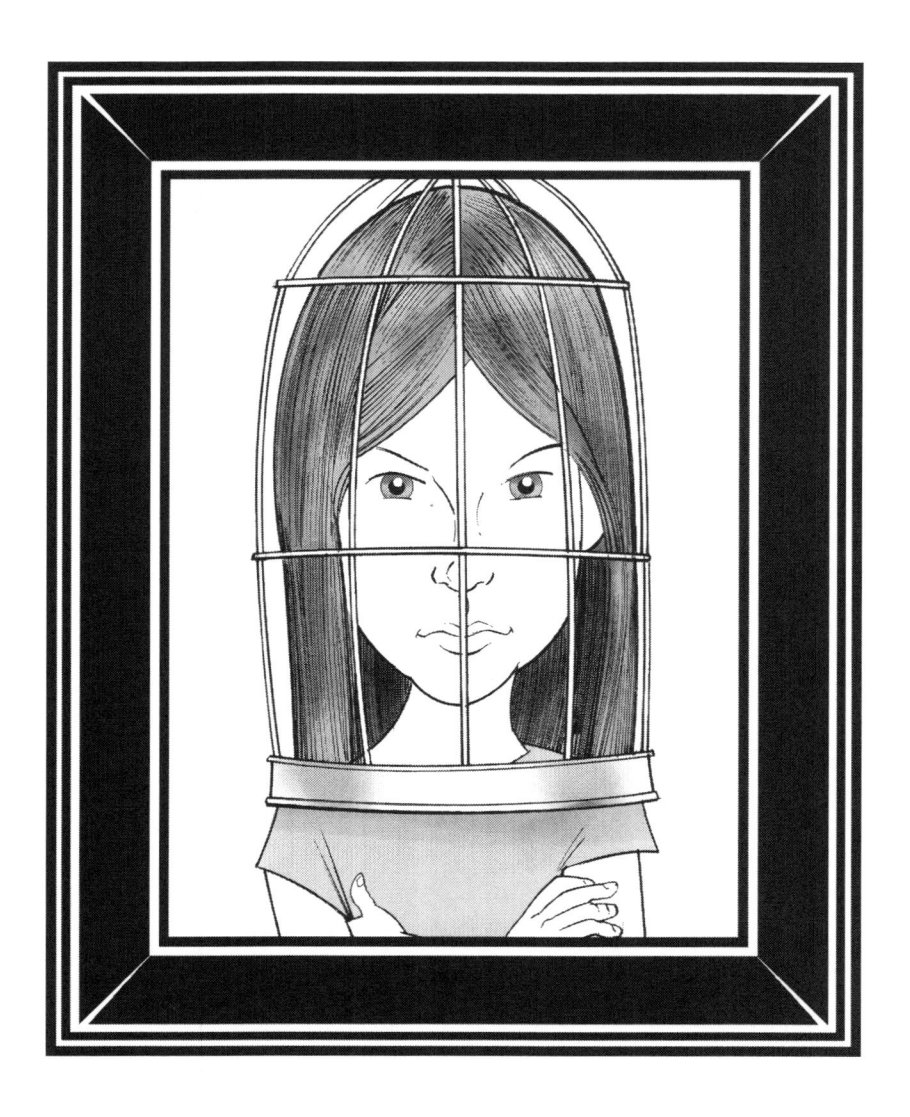

Birdie Motts

My mom won't let me have a pet. Go figure. She named me *Birdie*, for Pete's sake! OK, so that's just a nickname. My real name is Margaret Motts, but for some ungodly reason, Mom started calling me "Birdie" from the get go, and now it's stuck. But still. If she is so fond of birds, why won't she let me *have* one?

I get it about a dog. Yeah, we live in an apartment, and Mom works, and I am mostly in school all day. So a dog would be lonesome. Mom swears she is allergic to cats. I question this, since whenever I drag her into a pet store, she never once even so much as sneezes, and those places are *loaded* with cats. But I can live with the cat thing. But Mom also vetoed hamsters and gerbils on the grounds that they tend to escape and wreak all kinds of havoc. I kind of bought that argument, and really, rodents aren't my favorite.

But a nice, yellow, adorable canary? Or even better, a parrot—who could actually *converse* with you? Oh my gosh—how much fun would *that* be? I told my mom that there have been actual scientific studies done on the intellect of parrots and cockatoos. These studies indicate that the birds can solve intricate problems, and what's more, when their owners go into another room and think of a picture, let's say, of a *rose*, their birds, remember—*in another room*—say something appropriate, like "flower" or "blossom." Well, I guess you have to teach them to say "flower" or "blossom" first. Otherwise, it would be like a miracle or something.

But anyway, birds are easy. They stay in their cages, mostly. And if you want to let them out, they won't fly around the house, pooping all over—which is what Mom says. No—if you clip some crucial feather or something like that, they can't fly all over the place. They just flutter a little, and then settle down onto the perch you have thoughtfully provided. Then they just hang out, talk to you, and look gorgeous. And smart owners, of which I would be one, know to put a big towel or something under the perch. Then the poopage is manageable.

You can also hold your bird in your lap and pet it. I know this, because I have seen it on TV. This woman on Animal Planet has lots of birds, and really, they are just like lap dogs. That talk. I don't know how anybody could resist this. And they live a long time. So you don't have to deal with all that mourning after ten years or so. This mourning business is terrible. My best friend Clara's Golden Retriever died almost a year ago, and she still cries about it. But with a bird, you could have him all your life! Just think: if I got a parrot now, he could meet my children. And when I die, one of my kids would take care of him.

Mom reminds me that not everyone gets married. And then some married people never have children. She is a total killjoy. But I swear, I will keep at her until she caves.

Then I will get an African Grey parrot, and I will name it after my mother. Mildred Motts. Revenge.

Characters In Search of a Novel

Pasty Purvis

If you want to order a delicious cake, call Patsy Purvis. She has been baking them for years. I think someone said that she made her first one when she was four, but that may be an exaggeration. However, I have been buying her cakes for twenty years, and so I can attest to the fact that practice makes perfect.

Patsy Purvis' cakes are like heaven on a cake stand: light, deeply flavored, and never one bit dry. I would use the word "moist," but so many people cringe at that word; I don't know why. Her frostings are buttery, creamy, nice and thick, and frankly, I feel the cakes are simply the perfect vehicles for the frosting, which in my opinion is the main event.

Wouldn't you think Patsy would be chubby? Making all those cakes every day? She isn't. I would describe her as a freckled, well-endowed pillow of a woman. She has lovely hands. She wields a spatula like a magician! Her eyes are the color of chocolate buttercream, and she has a welcoming lap—that is, when she takes a little time to sit down. She has a rocking chair in her pantry, and she sits there and takes a little break. Patsy has a cup of tea in her rocker at around three in the afternoon, and she sips it while petting her Siamese cat,

Vanilla, who adores Patsy and her comfy lap. I would have to say that all in all, Patsy Purvis is as good as her cakes.

Patsy is married, naturally. We all know that the way to a man's heart is through his stomach. Carl Purvis gets a different kind of cake every night for dessert, and I can tell you this: he's a happy man. Carl drives the bus. He is very friendly to all of his passengers. Actually, that's how he met Patsy. She got on the bus one day after school, and they just kind of fell in love. Carl was twenty, and Patsy was eighteen. He was smitten even before he had one piece of cake. But after she served him his first slice of lemon pound cake, he was a goner.

Patsy and Carl live in a green and blue Victorian house with (naturally) gingerbread trim. The trim is all scallopy. Kind of like a wedding cake, if those were green and blue. It has a porch in the front, and in the back there is a gazebo. The gazebo looks a little bit like a cupcake.

Patsy hasn't gotten rich selling her cakes, but between her and Carl, they have just what they need. I guess you could say their life is like a fairy tale. But there is just one shadow in their lives, and it has caused them all kinds of grief and heartache.

Their daughter, Candice, gets hives if she eats sugar.

Characters In Search of a Novel

Little Randolph

Molly D. Campbell

Dear Dorcas,

I apologize for Randolph's behavior at your son's birthday party. I know how much thought and planning went into the event, and I am sure that it didn't even occur to you that some children are deathly afraid of clowns.

I have instructed Randolph to put on his "brave suit" when he is in situations that threaten him, but we didn't know that "Vlad the Dancing Clown" would be the featured entertainment at the party. So Randolph was caught by surprise when Vlad tried to pull him out of the audience to polka with him.

I certainly will pay for the Stanley Steemer people to remove the urine stains from your family room carpeting. And I had no idea that Randolph also managed to frighten Emma Pomeroy into doing the same thing in your kitchen. Luckily, you have high quality linoleum that cleans easily.

As regards to the birthday cake, I have chastised Randolph for spitting on some of the portions. He is a very sensitive child, and once he was "negatively aroused" by the dancing incident with Vlad, I'm afraid he lost some of his inhibitions, and "acted out." We are certainly going to have some serious sessions about this with our therapist, Melody Allgood.

Randolph is very sorry about any trouble that he might have caused. He has gotten over the case of hives that came on after he ate the pizza and grape Kool-Aid, followed by the fun-sized packages of M&Ms that were at each child's place. He tells me that the other children volunteered their candy, and that Gracie Teller's accusations of candy stealing were inaccurate.

We know that Randolph is a very special child. A boy with his high level of energy, coupled with his incredibly precocious intellect and personality make him extremely unique. We are proud of his talent for music, but once again, I am sorry that the other children did not enjoy his beat box rendition of "Happy Birthday." It is unfortunate that you had to administer the Heimlich Maneuver unnecessarily.

We would like to wish your son Dickie a most Happy Birthday. Randolph, my husband and I certainly hope that other than those few incidents, his party was a great success.

Sincerely,

Sabine Hemp-Wilder

Characters In Search of a Novel

Annie Withers

Annie Withers is dying of a broken heart. No, I really mean it. She has lost weight, there is absolutely no color in her cheeks, and she has bitten her once beautiful nails to the quick. A statuesque five foot nine, she now walks all slumped over like a dowager with that terrible hump. Osteoporosis. But Annie is only thirty-one.

The mortal mistake: Annie met the dark and mysterious Torvald Ren. He looks just like his name: he's tall but stringy, he has dull, lanky hair, but his eyes are the most intensely blue. And he rivets you with them. When I met him, it felt like he could see through my clothes to my underwear. But when he and Annie met, she instantaneously felt him look through her skin into her psyche. I know. I am shaking my head as I am telling you this.

Background. Annie Withers is lovely—or at least she was. She has a springy walk, firmly muscled arms and legs, and a distinct lilt to her voice. She wears leggings that make her legs look much longer, and she adores very high heels. She puts her long, thick hair into sometimes a bun, and sometimes a ponytail. Her eyes are amber. What can I say? She's a beaut.

Annie works alongside me at the newspaper. She writes about sports and entertainment. I write obits and the occasional tribute to a deceased scion or two. When work is over, we go out sometimes, and I try to pry any intelligence out of Annie as to how I should wear my hair, or whether it is worth using false eyelashes, what with all of the "ramp up" time it takes to learn how to put them on. Annie is a great teacher, and so far I have learned that you shouldn't wear a light top over dark bottoms unless you are in the petite range. Annie also instructed me about how to use concealer for dark under-eye circles. She is a font of information about beauty. Unfortunately for me, she is also beautiful, which makes her tutelage somewhat less valuable to me, since I am more in the "not homely, but not really that pretty" category.

I digress. Torvald Ren showed up in the newsroom one day, just kind of at random. Apparently he was on some sort of "temporary, international" assignment to cover the "Occupy Wall Street" activities from a foreign perspective. He was to study, interview, and then write brilliant observations about the American economy as a non-citizen. Which makes little sense to me, but hey—I write obits, as I said.

Tor (as he asked us to call him) began dogging Annie's heels, (high, as I mentioned) sniffing her perfume and saying charming things to her in his foreign accent like "You smell flower. No. You are flower." Ha ha. But she *thrived* on this stuff. And before any of us could say "NorwayorisitSweden?" he had her right where he wanted her.

So Annie and Tor became an item. They went to Finnish restaurants. She learned to like fishy bits in sour cream. They ate small pancakey things with dill and hardboiled eggs on them. Tor did get some color in his cheeks, but again—it didn't matter what the rest of his face looked like, because God graced him with eyes that could drop any woman at sixty paces.

Annie came in late more and more. This is really so predictable. She got happier and more vibrant. Tor, on the other hand, started making cracks about Annie's leggings, "Do American women wear skirts? Or is it something about your leg—have you a scar or embarrassment on the leg?" Of course, he knew the answer. They slept together from day one.

But we all worried that Annie wasn't picking up on the cues. She still smiled a lot, and brought that Norwegian/Danish/Finnish crisp bread for lunch, and continued to top it with stuff like fish and capers. She wore an occasional skirt, and one day she even wore *Danskos*, which she had always made fun of as "milkmaid clogs."

Meanwhile, Tor was getting around. He convinced Susie in Classifieds that she should write a novel. He told Marva Glenn in the Real Estate/Sunday Living department that she looked a lot like Ingrid Bergman. Marva had to Google that, but of course, she was thrilled beyond belief.

Things fell apart for Annie when she discovered Tor and Sygrid Nygaard together in the lunchroom, nearly breathing for one another. We all wondered why it took Tor so long to discover Sygrid, because really—don't birds of a feather tend to flock together?

So after Annie poured some Greek yogurt over Tor's head (no lutefisk was handy) and stormed out, she began to shake. Somebody noticed and told her to go home for the rest of the day.

We all thought someone as wonderful as Annie would bounce right back.

But here is the worry: she bites all the lipstick off her lips, and they are chappy and rough. She has some pimples. There are days when she comes to work in what looks like a nightgown, but she belts it at the waist, and probably before long it will be the latest style. But we all know that just because Annie can "pull off" wearing a nightgown with a red patent belt, that doesn't mean it's a good thing.

And Annie whines. Or maybe I should say, "Moans in a rather high register." So it sounds like she is having some sort of cramping pain as she types on her keyboard or sits in her cubicle in the ladies room.

We don't know what to do. This is like what happens in movies.

So where is George Clooney when you need him? If he could just come in for an interview with Claude in Entertainment, all might be well. Or maybe she should get a puppy. I am going to call her Mom, I swear.

Characters In Search of a Novel

Judith Jones

He looked non-threatening, for a therapist. She felt relieved about that. He motioned her to a seat on the suede sofa. She noticed that there were boxes of Kleenex on the end table and also on his desk. That was an omen. "Judith Jones, correct? Or would you prefer to be called Judy? I'm Dr. Young." Dr. Jung? She wondered if any of his other patients saw the inherent pun.

"Tell me everything about yourself. Don't leave anything out."

Oh, God. This was so exactly what she dreaded. "What do you want? Are you a Freudian?" She didn't want to mention Jung—too obvious. "Should I talk about my father? Or are you just fishing around for something hideous that we can get going on immediately?" He didn't respond but just raised his eyebrows.

"OK. So I am having anxiety. Let's just start there. My job is stressful, I am not in a relationship right now, and I bite my nails. My friends think I am obsessed with desserts. I have trouble sleeping. But I don't want to go over my entire life history. Is there a way to make this kind of quick?"

"Would you like to set a goal for your sessions here? Perhaps if we had an end point in mind, it would help you decide what you need to talk about when you are here."

She winced just slightly. "A goal? Like loving myself?"

He nodded. "Although that is just a bit ambitious. I think you might want to narrow that down a bit. Is there something more concrete you want to achieve? For instance, weight loss, or an improvement in a specific relationship?"

Good God. Now he was insinuating that she was *fat*. "Well, I have been having some anxiety lately."

He smiled. "What kinds of worries do you have?"

"Well, OK, I worry that I need to join Weight Watchers. But I just think the idea of weighing myself in public is horrendous. And I do keep a box of M&M's in my purse at all times." If he was thinking that she is going to just spill her guts voluntarily, he was woefully mistaken. She looked back at him.

"Well. You know, there are lots of groups out there who specialize in weight loss. I can recommend a few to you." He gave her a quizzical look.

She sighed. Obviously, she was going to have to *work* at this. "OK, OK. It isn't that. I know about Weight Watchers. Here's the thing." She paused. "I have trouble relating to men."

This got a little rise out of him. "I see. Do you mean that you have trouble communicating with men?"

This wasn't going to be easy. "Not really."

He frowned. "Lots of women find it hard to find balance in their relationships with men. Do you feel resentful towards men? Are you concerned with feminist issues?" He leaned forward, smiling. "Because these are common problems, and forging understanding between the sexes is a common topic for couples in therapy these days. We can do a lot to help men and women find common ground."

The clock was ticking. These sessions cost a lot, and she didn't want to waste the first one getting nowhere. It was obvious that she would have to just spill it. "Well, no. I guess I am a feminist, but I don't really want to find common ground with a man. When I say that I have trouble relating to men, I mean *relating* to men." She coughed, picked a lint speck from her jeans, and continued, "Actually, I am wondering if you can help me figure out if I am a lesbian."

He let out a small snort.

Characters In Search of a Novel

Marna Crosby

Marna Crosby was tired. Tired of looking out of the window while she cut up celery for lunch. Tired of bending over the washing machine, loading up sheets. Her head ached behind her eyes. She found herself sighing all the time.

She pictured her husband and children. Tess and Robby had nothing to think about but playing. They still skipped when they went down the driveway. Her husband Paul just stayed focused. He concentrated on the things that *mattered:* spreadsheets, the stock market, golf scores. He rarely had time to listen to Marna, even when she was upset.

It seemed as if the seasons just kept on changing. Nothing much happened to *her.* Marna's mother suggested that Marna look for a job that would be interesting, "After all, the kids are in school all day, and the house doesn't need every minute of your time!" Marna considered it, but she felt helpless and kind of stupid: she had never finished college, and she didn't really know how to do anything businesslike. So she scared herself out of looking at the classifieds or listening to those commercials for the local community college.

As she stared out of the kitchen window, she saw something moving—just out of the corner of her eye. She turned her head, and saw that it was a piece of purple yarn, somehow caught on the branch of the forsythia bush in the yard. The one they planted three years ago, that never seemed to want to bloom.

That's me, she thought. *Just stuck in the ground, not doing anything. Not growing, not blooming, not dying, nothing. Paul says it doesn't get enough sun. That we should move it. But who has time to go to all that trouble? To dig a hole, and then pull the thing out, and then dig another one to put it in? And who would fill the empty spot? With what? Another bush that wouldn't grow. And before we could do that, one of the kids would manage to fall in and get hurt.*

Paul had noticed that she was "sad." He told her to go out and "buy something fun, for heaven's sake." She had smiled when he said it, encouragingly, so that he would forget about it and pick up the paper again. But she didn't want anything, really. She didn't need anything. She just wanted to feel something inside. Right now she just felt nothingness.

Sometimes she would go to the mailbox, hoping for a surprise, something to change things. But nothing ever came, just bills and advertisements. She felt the same way sometimes when the phone rang: just the possibility of someone with news at the other end.

Marna knew that this would pass. She felt certain that if she took a vitamin or started taking walks, that her blood would start pumping again. Maybe if she got a puppy. Or there might be some kind of hormone that would help. Yes, that was it. She needed a boost. A physical, or a new hairdo, or maybe she should train for a marathon.

She looked out the window, and as she watched, a bird flew onto the forsythia and tried in vain to pull the shred of yarn from the branch. But it stayed put. The bird worried the yarn, shaking its head and backing up furiously. It was some sort of finch, Marna thought.

The little bird seemed to give up, rested, and then went at it again. No success. Finally, it flashed its wings in retreat. Marna grimaced. *At least I'm not alone.*

Scarlett Swells

She's a strumpet. This is not putting things mildly. She has held sway over men since she was old enough to bat her eyes. I think the entire second grade male population of P.S. 44 fell in love with her, and she has been going strong ever since.

You know how cosmetics are supposed to enhance a woman's sex appeal? Mascara, lipstick, and stuff? Scarlett never even uses powder. Her face looks perfect, and her eyes seem to gleam, even in the dark. How does she get her lips to be so pink? And no one calls those specks on her face *freckles*. Oh, no. Those little flecks just call out for men to touch her cheeks!

She doesn't even have red hair. I would call it dirty blonde, and that is the truth. But it looks better on her than the auburn hair on movie stars. Scarlet does that hair justice. I don't think she even uses curlers or anything. That hair just billows down around her shoulders. Those big green eyes don't hurt things, either.

Scarlet got a bust before the rest of us knew what a bra was for. And some of us still don't have hips we can swing around, but Scarlet knows how to strut. It is just unnerving the way men, including my brothers, salivate whenever Scarlet walks by.

Now it isn't fair to call her a strumpet without some proof. Well, I have seen her take money from men with my own eyes. And she doesn't *charge* them or anything. All she has to do is give them a kiss and they shower her with money and gifts. One time, she fainted *in church*, and the minister sent her flowers!

She has always had strings of boyfriends. Just stacks of them. The rest of us are lucky to get one at a time, but Scarlet needs a *schedule* for hers. One time she went to breakfast with one man, lunch with another one, and dinner with somebody else! And she has stayed in plenty of hotels, let me tell you.

I have discussed this with my mother. Mom says that Scarlet isn't that exceptional, really. Mom says that some people can write poetry, and some people can do math problems real fast. Scarlet can get men. It's a talent. We are all given talents. It's our job to figure out what our talents are and then develop them. Like Mom says that I have talent for growing things.

She says I would make a really good farmer or florist. And Scarlet just makes men want to give her things.

Here's the thing: I hate dirt. Here's another thing: I hate Scarlet. One more thing: I think Scarlet is going to marry my Daddy. After the divorce.

Characters In Search of a Novel

Algernon

She saw him out of the corner of her eye, trotting down the street. He ducked behind a building. Over the next few days, she saw him a number of times. He was gray, or maybe just filthy. He seemed to have a slight limp. His ears were floppy. He was very, very thin.

She started carrying dog biscuits in her purse. At first, she had to throw them to him so that he wouldn't flee. But after a while, she could hold one in her hand, and he would approach skittishly, and take it from her. By this time, she had named him "Algernon," and she was in love. It took a few weeks, but she could finally pet him.

In the meantime, she had been saving her money, and bit by bit, she bought some dog food, a little bed, a toy or two, and most importantly, a collar and leash. Algernon seemed to trust her, and each day, as she spoke softly to him, she petted him a bit longer. On a Friday, she put on the collar and leash, and she took him with her.

The vet told her that he was around two years old. He guessed that there was maybe some poodle and perhaps a bit of terrier in Algernon. He gave the dog shots, worming medicine, and a bath. As it turned out, Algernon was as white as snow.

She and Algernon became bosom buddies. They watched the neighborhood children play ball. They took lots of walks. Algernon seemed to enjoy donuts, and so they shared one every Friday, to celebrate the day they met. At home, they liked to read books, listen to Mozart, and look out the window.

Time went by, as it has the habit of doing, and Algernon slowed down a bit. He still liked to chase the occasional ball, but grew a bit stiff in the back end. She sometimes had to assist him up the steps. But he still sashayed with style, and she still thought he was the most beautiful dog in the world.

The day came as it always does. They had told her that Algernon would let her know when it was time to let go, and with one look into her eyes, he did. He went quietly and with his usual dignity, as she held him in her arms. She cried.

On her bureau is a framed picture of the dirty gray dog she befriended in the street. In it, he looks warily at the camera, the dog biscuit she has thrown at him at his feet. But there is a gleam in his eyes. Hanging over the corner of the frame is a blue leather dog collar. Embedded in the collar are the five remaining "jewels" that were on the collar when she bought it for him, that day that she decided she would take him home.

Characters In Search of a Novel

Amos Cargill

Well, he'd like you to think that he rode the range and punched the cattle. He looks a little leathery, but all those wrinkles come from smoking, not from squinting into the sun. He walks a little bowlegged, but his legs have never gripped the saddle.

Amos has watched all of the old Westerns, and he considers Matt Dillon and the Rifleman his kin. Amos has no brothers, and his sisters, Lily and Emily, don't understand why Amos is so obsessed with cowboys. When he was a kid, he took a pony ride at a birthday party and cried when the pony started to trot. But Amos liked the *idea* of being a cowboy so much that he just never gave it up.

Amos even named his sons Remington and Colt. His wife wouldn't let him name their daughter Kitty. She put her foot down on that one. And she lets Amos wear chaps around the house, but whenever they go out for errands, she makes him take them off. So he keeps a special hook for them in the front hall, right next to his lariat.

When friends come over for a cookout, you can be sure that Amos makes chuck wagon specialties, like beans with salt pork, coffee with eggshells, and hardtack. But his wife also serves hamburgers and potato salad. Amos never touches that stuff.

Amos has a riding mower. Natch. He has more fun on that thing! His wife hates how he tears up the lawn with it. And sometimes he "Yee haws" more than necessary. Amos wanted to put reins on the handles, but she also put a stop to that. And here's the thing: the Cargills' yard is mowed down to a nub in the summers, because Amos is out there riding the range on the damn thing twice a week!

I know all of this because the Cargills live on my street. When we first moved in, I happened to glance out the window and saw a cowboy doing rope tricks in the yard a few houses down. He was wearing fancy snakeskin boots, a red neckerchief, and those chaps. My wife said, "Oh, that's Amos Cargill; he thinks he's the Lone Ranger or something. I hear he's very harmless, and pretty charming, actually. But if we get invited over there, don't eat *anything* he cooks. Stick with the stuff his wife brings out."

So Amos and I are great friends now. We talk shop, and he shows me the stuff he buys at tack sales: bits, spurs, and a stirrup or two. He has an old saddle mounted on a sawhorse in his garage, and he gets on it and fools around a little. It's all in good fun.

Sometimes he comes over to my house, and we look at my collection of antique parasols and beaded shawls. Amos thinks they are pretty. He is the picture of good manners. When I put on my beauty mark and wig, and a little make-up, and ask him how I look, he says, "Why, Miss Kitty, you look sublime."

Yep. We're just two old buddies, out in our garages, talking hobbies. Amos, the cowboy dermatologist, and Christopher, the cross-dressing electrician.

Characters In Search of a Novel

Mimsy Carrothers

To Whom It May Concern:

My name is Mimsy Carrothers. I am ten, but most people think that I am in my teens. I'm that precocious. My mother says that I am going to send her to an early grave, and since she says it all the time, it has gotten me started thinking about dying, myself. My Gram told me that when you get old enough to die, you leave your Last Will and Testament so that your family will know what to do with your important things. I asked Gram, "Important things like what?" And she said it was stuff like papers, stocks and bonds, and money.

I don't have any of that stuff. I don't know what it is. So I asked Gram what I should do. Gram said, "Well, Mimsy, do you feel that you are drawing close to death?" I thought about it, and said that I don't really think so, but now that I know that you have to have a will, so that people will know what to do with your stuff, I worry a lot about my important stuff.

So Gram told me to get some nice, thick paper, a good rollerball pen, and write down what I want to do with my stuff.

Gram says you choose the people you love the most to give your things to, and that you mustn't forget charity and the poor. So I spent yesterday thinking about my things, the poor, and dying. It was creepy. So here is:

<u>Mimsy Carrothers' Last Will and Testament</u>

1. I want to leave my Mom and Dad all my underwear and pajamas. They smell like me if they haven't been washed yet, and I think they will like smelling them.

2. I also, since I am on the subject of pjs, would like for my Dad to have all my sneakers. He might like smelling them. I don't think Mom would.

3. To my brats for brothers, I leave all the old Halloween candy in the bag in my closet. It's kind of grotty, but Snotface and Fartsforbreath will eat anything.

4. To my Gram, I leave my necklace with the heart on it, because inside are her picture on the left and my Mom's picture at her wedding to Dad on the right. I think Gram will like this.

5. All my stuffed animals I donate to charity. I think poor kids would like them. I never play with them anymore,

and they really just lay around in the corner of my room in a big basket. So I think they would be appropriate for poor children everywhere.

6. In my savings account, I have my college fund, set up by Gram and Grandpa before Grandpa died. I think it has a lot of money in it. The reason it has a lot of money in it is that Dad keeps putting money in it whenever he wins at poker. So I want to give that money to my Dad and Mom, to pay them back for putting up with what the "Dear Abby" column calls "adolescent anks" or something like that. Parents hate the anks.

7. For my two friends Stephania and Merrillee, I leave all my makeup. I have some really good Hello Kitty stuff, and my sister Caroline gave me some mascara and nail polish samples that I haven't tried yet.

8. My main problem is my iguana, Reginald. Nobody in my family likes him. They think he's gross. So I guess I have to leave him to Mr. Cohen, my science teacher. I hope Mrs. Cohen likes Reginald, because he is really sweet, and he loves to be petted. We watch movies together, while I eat popcorn and Reginald has some

salad. Mrs. Cohen: Don't give Reginald salad with <u>dressing</u> on it, or he'll get sick and die. Mrs. Cohen, you can also have his aquarium and heat light, and the shavings so he can pee in them.

9. I hate my sister Caroline mostly. But she is nice to me on average once every month. So for that (thanks for nothing) and for not hitting me on the back of the head any more, I leave Caroline my Uggs that she wears all the time anyway, my glitter hair extensions, and my three best pairs of shin guards. Caroline plays field hockey. She should be happy to have a few spares.

10. To my brothers who are obnoxious and smell bad, I leave my deodorant. I only use it after gym class.

11. Finally, to Gram, since she told me how important it is to have a last will and testament, I leave my Pandora bracelet (but it only has two charms. One of a frog and a red and yellow bead). I think Gram will like adding to it over the rest of her life.

12. Please put some flowers on Grandpa's grave for me once in a while.

13. To Mom and Dad. Don't be sad that I died young. They say that the good die young. Since you tell me every day to be good, especially before I get out of the carpool for school, then I must have been *very* good to be dead right now. That should make you both happy.

14. I would like now to say goodbye to Reginald, Gram, Grandpa, Mom and Dad, Snotface (OK, Brian) and Fartsforbreath (OK, Daniel), Caroline (you should never have pulled my hair like that) and my friends Merillee, Stephania, Madison, Lauren, and Bobo (well, her parents named her Barbara).

15. I guess I got some sort of really bad disease, or a terrorist shot me at the mall, or I got that poisoning you get from eating food at school when the pie lady forgets to wash her hands after she pees. Whatever it was, it struck me down in my prime. Or before my time. But remember, all of you that I was really good to die at my young age. That should make you all feel better.

Signed, Mimsy Carrothers aged 10

Witness: Eleanor Garrison, age 77 (Gram)

Characters In Search of a Novel

Sergeant Winteregg

This guy is in for it. How come he joined the academy? No cop named "Winteregg" will survive one *minute* in the streets! And what are the rest of us supposed to call him? "Hey Eggie!" or "Winnie?" It won't cut it. His first name isn't any better. *Alvin*? My God, I think the guy has a death wish!

I have to admit that the kid is buff. But with a name like Alvin Winteregg, you would have to be. And get this: he doesn't even want us to call him *Al*. He says that using his full name is just fine.

So we are out there on the street, and some big, burly kid comes running out of an alley carrying a bag of money, drugs, or something, and I am supposed to shout, *"Cover Me, Alvin?"* It just might work—the kid might bust a gut laughing. I asked around, and all of us are in complete agreement that this guy is totally unreal! He's nice, he follows directions OK, and he can hold his own in a terrorist drill. He can shoot a gun and hit the target. But what gives with the name? Interrogations? No way: "Well, you better talk, or I will be forced to call in Sergeant Winteregg?" Are you kidding?

In my mind, his mother must have wanted him to be a librarian or a poet or something. And then ol' Alvin just turned macho on her. She must have wanted him to take piano lessons and learn how to make bread, but instead he asked her for karate lessons and a raw egg mixed in milk. I bet his mom winced every time ol' Alvin farted in the house.

But to honor his pansy-assed mom, Alvin promised her that he wouldn't call himself Al, is all I can figure. I bet he sure hated that Chipmunks record that came out. And I also can imagine that Alvin's father, probably Oswald or Percy or something like that, supported ol' Alvin's mother. He probably wanted Alvin to wear suspenders or something.

The more I think of it, the more I kind of feel sorry for ol' Alvin. Shit, maybe he's tougher than me! Or Mike! Or Bull, for God's sake. Alvin might be kind of like that guy named "Sue," that Johnny Cash sang about. But I bet even "Sue" had a normal *last* name! I wonder if Alvin has a hot wife named Brandi or Karlene or something. Wait: "Brandi Winteregg...." Naw. Her name is probably something like Clementine, and she plays the ukulele or the harmonica or sings opera songs. I bet she has a big chest and wears muumuus.

Molly D. Campbell

Alvin Winteregg. I wonder what his *middle* name is.

Characters In Search of a Novel

Wilma Trickles

Behind her Coke bottle spectacles, Wilma's eyes are lively, brown and bulging. They don't really bug out, but the glasses make it look that way. Wilma has about a million freckles, and she tends to blush a lot. But don't let anything like that fool you: Wilma may be homely, but inside, she's a beauty.

For instance. When Wilma was ten, some boys were in back of the drugstore, and they had a cat cornered. I can't even say what they were doing; it's too ugly. But Miss Wilma heard the howling, and she went out there and one by one, *kicked their asses*. Then she took the cat home and named him Lucky.

Wilma works at the pharmacy, filling orders and waiting on customers. I guess you could say she's a "pharmacy tech." She might as well be the pharmacist, for all she knows. She saved Harvey Smith's life—only Wilma noticed that the drugs he was taking for his heart, combined with the new drugs he was prescribed for his gout, were lethal together. And she can tell you what you need for itching, coughing, sour stomach, and the best over-the-counter ways to prevent pregnancy. She's a real boon to everybody in town.

Wilma has a boyfriend. He's not much to look at, either. But Gil Dilworth is the best piano player around here. He is always in demand for weddings, church affairs, and even parties—if you happen to have a grand piano at your house, and you want to have fifty people over, ask Gil to provide "cocktail music." He only charges $35 a night.

Gil and Wilma might get married. I don't know. Wilma lives at home with her mother, who depends on Wilma way too much, if you want to know my opinion. I bet Gil would be fine living with Wilma and her mother, but I think Wilma is doubtful about that. It's the same old story: woman dotes on mother, takes care of her until it's too late to have a life of her own. But nobody can tell Wilma anything, and she is devoted to her Ma.

But I heard something. My mother goes to book club with Gil's brother's wife, Patty. My mom said that Patty said that Gil said something about getting "sick and tired." I think that's what Mom said that Patty said that Gil said. So. Something big may be happening.

Either that, or Gil needs some vitamins.

Molly D. Campbell

Characters In Search of a Novel

Veronica Stabbs

Once more, I am seething. This time, Veronica topped *herself*. I mean, really. We all know that she operates completely "above the law," but when it comes to fund-raising art auctions for the good of the community at large, I just somehow thought Ronnie Stabbs would behave herself.

She has a history of arranging things so that they come out just the way she wants them to. I think she blackmailed her mother into buying her that expensive beaded prom dress. She has *something* on just about everybody in her family, and believe me, Ronnie *uses* it. And in school, her unfortunate male teachers fell under the spell of her false eyelashes frequently, which is why she won the science prize for a model of how gingivitis develops in people who don't floss. Her dad, Grant Bleeth, D.D.S., made the model for her—we all knew that. And to top it all off, it was extremely realistic, and it made many of the people who looked at her exhibit kind of queasy.

Ronnie is what men like to call "luscious." She is what women like to call "a bitch." She has long, red hair that she puts up in a Grace Kellyesque chignon. It's so fifties, but boy, men just drool. So naturally, she was able to captivate Brent Stabbs immediately. She wore his frat pin proudly on her left boob, and then ended up with a two-carat emerald cut—engaged, her senior year at Wellesley, where she probably cheated on all her exams.

The wedding was predictable: Alençon lace (gown by Vera Wang), eight bridesmaids, all of whom secretly hated the bride, and a raw bar and lobster dinner for three hundred. Imagine—three hundred people. Must have been mostly from the groom's side.

Brent, naturally, is an attorney. So he has to be social. And on his arm, Ronnie sparkles. Or tries to--with her white veneers; Botoxed forehead; shellacked, fire engine red nails; Jimmy Choos; and, probably, long-line Spanx.

You think I am sounding a little bitter? I have a right to. Here are just a few things Ronnie has shoved me out of the way to get: The science prize (I made my own display about erosion, and spent many an hour in the basement, dribbling water down those goddamned hills—one covered with grass and one bare); Tommy Reeder, who never knew Ronnie stuffed her bra; the perfect attendance prize in eighth grade (she paid her twin sister to come to homeroom for her when Ronnie had cramps, sheesh); Brent, who happened to ask me out on three dates before he met Ronnie and her eyelashes; the coveted "Halloween Homeroom Mom" assignment (it's the easiest one; all you have to do is show up with a crap load of candy); and now, tonight, she committed the sneakiest crime in her nefarious career of sneakiness.

Silent Auction. Donations from tip-top sources all over town. To support the local Special Olympics, for heaven's sakes. There were tons of good items: Weekends at B & Bs, massages, a set of pretty attractive Corelle dinnerware, a year's supply of kibble, and what I really had my eye on: a complete beauty make-over, including eyebrow threading, microdermabrasion, nail shellacking, and a whole lot of other great stuff: a day of beauty.

First of all, I need this. I am not particularly stunning. Ronnie Stabbs does *not*. She has weekly massages, and her lips are stuffed with her own ass fat, or something equally expensive. She has blue contacts, not one single discernible pore, and she looks like January Jones, for Pete's sake.

So I put in a bid of $250 five minutes before the silent auction ended, and I *stood right by the table to make sure that my name was the last one on that infernal sheet!*

But I should have known. Veronica Stabbs, who more than lives up to her name, arranged to be the person who collected all the sheets to give them to the committee who tallied up everything. And you know what happened: Ronnie Stabbs won the day of beauty.

This will catch up to her. Because I am starting a secret society. And our goal is to bring down Ronnie Stabbs. I am drawing up a list of members. Our secret handshake is going to be, "Bat your eyelashes three times, wag your ass, and then make a 'stabbing' motion straight towards the heart of the person you are greeting." That's all I have, so far.

This may be my life's crowning achievement....

Molly D. Campbell

Characters In Search of a Novel

Duke Devlin

I met him at a cocktail party. He was quite breathtaking, really—bronzed arms, those dazzling azure eyes, and the mole right above his left eyebrow. His hair was as black as coal—I know, how trite can one description be? But I was awestruck. And when he put out his hand for me to shake and said, "Hello, there. My name is Devlin. My first name is Benjamin, but for some reason, they call me Duke," I was instantly in love.

He offered me a drink, and when I asked for vodka with lemon, he obliged. We struck up a conversation, and I found myself telling him things that I would normally not admit to my best girlfriends, much less a total stranger. He said he was a writer, and suddenly everything fell into place: the arresting demeanor, the probing questions, and the penetrating gaze. It was like the fairy tales; before I knew it, the night was over.

I didn't see much of him in the weeks afterward. My hostess informed me that Duke traveled the world, doing research for his books. Apparently, after the evening we met, he left for Africa for an extended safari. Then I heard that he was in the South of France, then Italy.

The world turns. Things go on. I changed jobs myself, and met a very nice young man who sold pharmaceuticals. He and I saw a lot of each other, and married a few months later. We moved to the suburbs, had two lovely children, and became busy with diapers, yard work, and budgets—the normal occupations for young marrieds.

I never really forgot Duke Devlin, although sometimes it seemed as if I had made him up. After all, there was just that one brilliant night spent in the company of someone so different from the rest of the people in my life.

Four years ago, I heard the news. Duke Devlin was coming back into town. There was to be a celebration of the literary kind, involving guest writers or something—I don't really know. I had hoped to attend the speech that he was to give, but my seventeen-year-old daughter got herself into some trouble at an unsupervised party at her best friend's house, and she was grounded. I felt I had to stay home to supervise. Oh, yes, I guess I forgot to mention that I divorced my husband when the children were small. He wasn't as nice as he seemed.

I looked for Duke's picture in the paper the next day, but I didn't see anything. I heard that his speech was riveting. Of course, it would be. It was crushing, really, not to see him once again. I reminded myself that life isn't a movie, and I put the paper down and picked up a dust cloth.

But then the phone rang. I answered it, and the breath was simply sucked right out of my chest. "Hello, Sally? Do you remember me? It's Duke. Duke Devlin. We met many years ago."

The rest is history. We arranged to meet at "The Suave Pig," a local nightspot. I wore way too much make up, a girdle, and just in case, it had lace on it. He looked a bit dissipated, with graying hair that showed a lot of scalp underneath, a bit of a paunch, and of all things, he wore brown Hush Puppies. We didn't hit it off quite as electrically that time. It was a huge disappointment for both of us.

We just celebrated our second wedding anniversary.

Marla Swaine

She walks in beauty. I know; that's not a bit original. But it's true. Miss Swaine was born with sea blue eyes, gracefulness, a soft voice, and the clearest, most gleaming complexion you have ever seen. Her hair is the color of caramel apples. And I think she smells like cinnamon.

Marla Swaine is my teacher. My name is Albert Moses. Nobody thinks anything about me. I just have pimples and sit in the back of the class. Miss Swaine teaches us all about poetry and the great writers. Her favorite is a man named D. H. Lawrence, and she says that maybe when we are in college, we can read his books. Miss Swaine says that they aren't appropriate for the seventh grade. She says that there is a whole world out there, just waiting for us.

Miss Swaine told me that I shouldn't worry about my face or anything else physical. She says that a true poet resides in my soul. She knows about things like that, being that she is an expert in literature and stuff. See, I keep a notebook, and I write my thoughts down. I never let anybody look at it, but one time I showed Miss Swaine parts of it. She told me that the way I described sunset, "like the sky was fierce and feverish," was like a poem. She told me that I should start to write stories and verses. So now I do.

I asked Miss Swaine why the popular kids are so cruel to the rest of us. And she told me that it's because all of us are really scared inside. I asked her what she meant, and she said that even beautiful people feel all alone sometimes, and that just about everybody is afraid of what their lives might bring. I asked her what she was afraid of, and she said, "Albert, I am afraid that my children won't think of me as anything but their mother." I don't really understand that, but it made me feel good to know that Miss Swaine is just as uneasy as I am inside.

Miss Swaine isn't even married, and yet she worries about what her children will think of her. That is a wonder to me. If I had a mother as beautiful and gentle as Miss Swaine, I would think the whole world of her. My mother is good, and I love her, but she has never once thought about the sunset as anything but what comes before it gets dark. My mother is too busy for anything like poems or D. H. Lawrence. But then again, one time my mother was Miss Swaine's age. I wonder if she worried about what I would think of her, once I was born.

Molly D. Campbell

I am going to ask her.

Characters In Search of a Novel

THE CAT LADY

You asked me what is the scariest thing I have ever known? That is easy to tell you. When I grew up, I lived in Cabotville, that village just outside of Easton, way up in the northern part of the state. You know—not a big place—about three hundred folks lived there when I was growing up in the early 1950s.

There was nobody had money then, not in Cabotville. Most of our families just ate what they grew. What came up was what you had. And a few scrawny chickens, if you had good luck. So we grew up. Nothing but scabbed knees, dirty hands, and that raw look on our faces—the look that hungry people get used to.

I think somebody said her name was Junifer or something. She lived in a filthy place not even the tough ones visited. Momma never knew how this Junifer got any money, but she existed somehow. She ate what she scrounged out of her weedy back yard, I guess. But the real mystery is that Junifer had cats. Lots of 'em. By high count, one year, they say she kept thirty of 'em on her property. There was always about ten of those cats slinking around the dust in the Cat Lady's front yard. We called her the Cat Lady. Everybody did.

Them cats weren't too good looking, but neither was she. They had the mange, some of 'em, and others looked skinny and lame. The worst ones had scummy eyes and noses. Most of 'em were wild as they come. But one or two would let you pet 'em, but no one wanted to—they were so puny. The Cat Lady had wall eyes, sparse hair, and a big red scar running down her left cheek. So she was a lot like those cats. Maybe that's why nobody messed with her.

Well, the Cat Lady loved all of 'em. She boiled up what looked like rats and oatmeal for 'em, and she kept 'em alive, that's something. The Cat Lady would sit on the stoop, with one of them sick ones on her lap, and she'd sing to it and pet it like it was her baby. It might just be that Junifer, the Cat Lady, was a little touched.

Well, nothing ever ends well for crazy people in small towns. One Sunday, after church, they caught the Cat Lady going through the trash in back of the Superette, looking for scraps. That weren't too bad, but they say that Junifer hardly had any clothes on. It was a hot day and all, but they say that she wasn't covered enough to be in her right mind, you know. So they called the county, and the next week, some Socialists, or some such name, came for the Cat Lady, and took Junifer away.

No one did anything for those cats. Like I say, I was awful young back then, and I don't recollect what happened to all of 'em. But don't you figure they just starved and died? I think people who cart people off and let their cats die are downright scary, don't you?

Course, my momma took five of them cats....

.

Characters In Search of a Novel

Farley Spratt

If you think you have seen it all, you haven't. Farley Spratt <u>has</u>. He drives a cab from the airport to all the downtown hotels and back, and believe me, he has the stories. Farley went to barber school, but he soon discovered that all that hair flying around made him sneeze. And although he loved making conversation with strangers, standing up all day inflamed his bunions. So when he saw the ad in the classifieds that All City Cabs was hiring, Farley went in, and he got the job.

There was a test he had to pass, though. Farley stayed up nights studying the street map, and his wife Arlene quizzed him on it. She'd say, "Now Farley, take me from the airport to the Holiday Inn on Fairmore Street," and Farley would have to tell her what route he'd choose. But he had to know the way to all sorts of places around town, just to pass the test. So Arlene would ask him to take her from Dart's Hunting and Fishing Emporium over to Dr. Marcia Horstman's office—and she's a gynecologist, so Farley really had to study up on that one.

He passed the test with flying colors, thanks to Arlene. And wouldn't you know it? His first fare asked him to take her from the airport to, of all places, the cemetery out on Flinger Avenue, way out in the sticks. And she made Farley wait while she put little pots of fake geraniums on three graves.

There are other stories that are even more interesting. Farley says that he took a group of rappers on a tour of the city, because they were "bored." He had a hard time understanding them, but he got the gist. They asked him to take them to the best club in town. So Farley dropped them off at The Blue Light. They gave him a *hundred dollar tip.*

Somebody once left a valise full of drugs in the back of his cab. Or so Farley thought. He took it to the police station, where all the cops just laughed at Farley for being so suspicious. It was *Timothy Hay.* Turns out that fare was a rabbit breeder, coming to town to pick up a couple of French Lops.

Farley's most exciting trip, though, was when the sexy blonde woman and what looked like her "boy toy" got into the cab and told Farley to take them to the four star hotel with the private pool on the roof. They kept up pretty hot and heavy in the back seat all the way there, and Farley almost had a wreck from looking in the rear view. By the time they arrived at the hotel, the bellman got an eyeful! Turns out the woman was Madonna, or Lady Gaga or somebody like that—Farley isn't sure. And guess what? The woman didn't leave a tip *at all*. I guess she was too busy trying to hide the fact that she wasn't wearing underpants.

Arlene is glad that Farley is a cabbie. Because she saw on "60 Minutes" or somewhere that cab drivers almost never get Alzheimer's. It has something to do with all that memorizing. It keeps their minds really sharp, and they just keep their wits about them all their life. It's a relief to Arlene, because she has started forgetting where she put her glasses. Farley can take care of her if she starts to lose it. So Arlene knows that she won't have to put any big deposits down on one of those "memory care" places. The Spratts will be fine, staying right where they are.

Characters In Search of a Novel

The Maestro

My father was far from ordinary. Other children's dads were doctors, lawyers, and teachers. Their dads went to work in the morning and came home for dinner. Their dads played golf on the weekends. My father was a maestro.

I grew up hearing him play the violin, beautifully. He had a lovely one, with real gold on the pegs, and also on the bow. It had a beautiful velvet-lined case, with little pockets for rosin and extra strings. There was a silk-lined velvet blanket to cover the violin. When he played, I used the case as a doll bed.

I grew up in concert halls, sitting very quietly during rehearsals, where my father stood on a big podium in front of the orchestra, waving his arms. Everyone in the orchestra seemed in awe of my Dad. I thought it was because he was so handsome. But I knew he was the boss of all of those musicians, and I was very proud.

When my father went to work, it was at night. After an early dinner, he would get dressed. I loved this ritual. First the beautiful white shirt with all the little pleats. Pearl buttons. Black pants with a satin stripe down the sides. Cummerbund.

Dad had a few different pairs of cufflinks, and I got to choose which ones he wore. I felt so important. Then the shiny patent leather shoes. And finally, the tails and bow tie, which he tied himself. He was a glorious man.

I hated actually going to see him conduct, because those evenings were long and boring. I got tired of watching him in front of the orchestra after about five minutes. My mother had made it clear that there was to be no twitching, no neck craning, and no noise. I perfected this, but for years afterwards, I hated going to concerts, remembering the constraints of childhood!

My father was magnificently handsome. He was tall, dark, and charming. He was the object of many women's fantasies, and I think indulged many of them. It made me cherish him all the more, because I think in my childish subconscious, I was afraid one of his admirers might carry him away from us.

The maestro was my biggest fan. He thought I was beautiful when I had pimples. He was the first person to tell me that I should be a writer. He was never too busy to hug, or to listen.

We watched "The Tonight Show" together every weeknight. He concocted very interesting late night snacks.

The Maestro died when I was a young mother. I wish I could go to just one more concert. I wouldn't move a muscle.

Characters In Search of a Novel

Florian Muenster

Oh, my gosh. You haven't seen his rose garden? I can't believe it. It's locally famous, on the corner of Genoa Avenue and Hill Streets. The corner lot. You can drive right past it and see just about everything, but if you want a tour, just ring the doorbell, and Mr. Muenster will walk you through it. Funny name, right? It makes you think of that old gothic TV show?

Florian Muenster is the nicest, least scary person in the entire world. He came over here as a kid with his parents during WWII, because they couldn't stand what was going on in their homeland. So I guess that proves that the Germans weren't "unaware" of what Mr. Hitler was up to! Belton, Florian, and Hulda Muenster moved in to the little house on that corner, and thought they didn't have much, they worked very hard. Hulda took on domestic duties in some of the larger homes around town, and Belton did all kinds of things: he tuned pianos, played flute in the local orchestra, and he could fix almost anything. Florian worked hard in school and had four paper routes. And he and Belton did odd jobs for the same folks that Hulda cleaned for. They saved their money.

Florian was their only child, and my parents say that he used to work in the corner garden alongside his mother in all weathers. They grew not only roses, but they had a "victory garden," and they were very generous. Mother says that their tomatoes made the very best juice. I hate tomato juice, so I can't imagine.

When Florian was in high school, he won all kinds of scholastic awards, and so he got a full scholarship to college. I think he went to Boston University, but I am not sure. He came back to town when his father died, and he stayed with his mother until she died. He was a good son, and he never got married. He just kept Hulda company, nourished those lovely roses, and smiled at friends and strangers alike.

When his father died, Florian was depressed for a while. He let weeds grow in the yard, and all the neighbors were worried. But then he snapped out of it, and things went on as usual.

Florian Muenster must be in his eighties by now. Maybe older—I am not sure. I saw him in his yard just the other day. He was wearing a straw hat, gardening gloves, and overalls.

The sun was shining, and he squinted through his bifocals at me, and then smiled and said, "Why, hello, liebchen!" And he cut a yellow rose, and offered it to me.

I hope he never dies.

Characters In Search of a Novel

Rachel Klenhauser

She never quite outgrew the awkward stage. It began at around age nine, when Rachel started shooting up, and by the time she was in junior high, she was taller than most of the tallest boys. Rachel had long legs and an even longer waist, which made her dresses cinch up just under her rib cage. That frustrated her mother no end, because Rachel had to wear a dress to school every day. This was in the late 1950s, way before the women's liberation movement was a gleam in Betty Friedan's eye.

Rachel wore glasses, too. Her first pair that she got in third grade were "cat glasses" with white frames with glitter in them. Rachel's mom convinced her that they were "all the rage." After that, Rachel no longer trusted her mother's opinion about *anything.*

Rachel and her best friend, Marie Dorfley, were both smart. This did nothing for their popularity. While they held up their hands, signaling the right answer, their classmates rolled their eyes and made farting sounds in their armpits. After school, Rachel and Marie walked home together, for security reasons.

Rachel had a bit more luck in high school, when contact lenses became popular. She convinced her mom to let her have them.

Unfortunately, the hard lenses were very difficult for Rachel's eyes to accustom to, and so Rachel squinted her way through her junior and senior years. Sunlight also bothered her contact-lensed eyes, and Rachel carried a Kleenex at all times, for watering and sneezing purposes.

Rachel never had a boyfriend until she went to college. At Northwestern, where she had a full ride, Rachel began to get with it. Her roommate freshman year, Holly Finn, taught Rachel to put perfume behind her knees and between her breasts. Holly also showed Rachel how to stand up straight in order to show off her entire frontal area, including the perfumed breasts, long legs, and small (albeit long) waist.

During her senior year at Northwestern, Rachel tried out for a production of "A Midsummer Night's Dream," and to her surprise, she was cast as Hippolyta. She triumphed! For the first time, Rachel wasn't awkward, she was an Amazon! It changed her life.

There were some talent agents in the audience. They often scout prominent theatre schools, looking for potentials. Rachel had potential in spades. The agents had a little confab with

Rachel after the play, and one of them gave her his card. Rachel put it in her billfold, and the rest is history.

Oh yes, she changed her name. You may have seen her. She became famous in New York on the stage, and made a few movies. There are thousands of people in her fan clubs. She has a stage name and a chauffeur.

But Rachel still remembers that day senior year, when she tripped over her own feet in the cafeteria and spilled spaghetti and meatballs all over the football team. In her mind, she is one misstep away from humiliation. One wrong step.

Characters In Search of a Novel

Mom and Ida

Ida's parents lived through the Depression. That generation of people were branded by the experience. Ida grew up watching her mother use every last teaspoon of batter, save even one sip of milk, and keep everything from used newspapers to rubber bands. So Ida learned how to economize.

Ida says that we throw way too much away these days. She frets when she sees her friends eat a chicken dinner and throw away the bones. "They are discarding the makings of delicious soup!" she cries. And I have seen the stockpot on the back of Ida's stove, and I have tasted her broth. It is something to write home about.

Except I can't really write home about it, because Ida is my aunt. She lives in our neighborhood, three doors down. And my mother is one of the people that Ida despairs over—my mother is the one who throws away her chicken bones. There is a difference between Ida and my mother: Ida was the oldest of four children, and by the time my mother came along, the Depression was a bit more of a memory. Ida witnessed people living within a strict budget and making a good life in spite of it. My mother just perceived two silly old parents who hoarded things and preached too much about money.

Not that my Mom is a spendthrift or anything. She sews most of our clothes and doesn't throw her money around. But if there is a tiny bit of spaghetti sauce left, Mom pitches it. If Ida sees her, she says things like, "But you could add that to meatloaf and improve the taste! Why are you wasting it?" My mom just shrugs, and throws it in the trash anyway.

But it's funny. My mother would never in a million years spend money on an expensive vacation. But Aunt Ida has gone on three cruises with Uncle Paul. Ida says that after all these years, they deserve to "live it up a little." Mom says that if Ida wouldn't worry so much about wasting things, she wouldn't *need* to live it up.

Lately, Ida has gotten worse. She says that nobody needs to get new clothes every year, and that it's a sin the way people drive all over creation, wasting gas at these prices. Mom agrees, but I know for a fact that she and Dad still like to take Sunday drives, just to see the sights—even though it's a waste of gas.

I guess it's a matter of the way people look at things. Mom thinks that life is worth savoring at home, and that saving a tablespoon of spaghetti sauce is "false economy." Aunt Ida thinks that we should never forget the Great Depression, and that the reason so many people are poor and suffering today is because they don't know how to stretch a dollar.

I think that Ida's meatloaf is delicious, and the perfect thing to do after dinner is go for a ride in the country. I am not exactly sure what that makes me....

Hester Packmore

Let's face it. Hester isn't exactly slim. She refers to herself as "healthy." She has said on more than one occasion that people spend way too much time worrying about their looks. "A good ten or so extra pounds will serve you in good stead if you get sick," she says. I see her point, but I also have to say that Hester has enough extra for a bout with pneumonia, a case of shingles, and an abscessed tooth. Hester has been my best friend for twenty years.

Hester loves desserts. She makes the best strawberry shortcake in the world. Here is the trick: warm shortcakes, drenched with butter, and *juicy* strawberries. "Nothing worse than dry shortcake! And why people stint on the whipped cream is a mystery to me." I agree. Just about nobody puts butter on the shortcakes first. Also, Hester knows how to make the most delicious buttercream frosting. Once again, the trick is to *make a double recipe and put a lot on*. For some reason, people think it's fashionable to just dab a little of it on. Hester won't even order dessert in a restaurant, for this very reason: they are stingy with everything. "If I ordered double topping or extra frosting, they would look at me like I have some sort of disease. I would rather just go home and have brownies or some ice cream, for Pete's sake."

Hester had her physical six months ago, and the doctor told her she had to lose about thirty pounds, or else she would get a "fatty liver." Now, that sounds awful. I think it gives you high blood pressure or something. So Hester has been on a diet, and I tell you right now, she's turned ugly. Like Satan. I'll give you an example: last week, when we were at the mall, she just about blew up at me when I suggested that we stop for one of those hot pretzels. She accused me of sabotage. Whew! I told her I didn't know what I was doing—you know, temporary insanity. She bought it, and I got off the hook. But I just have to stay on my toes in the food department. Well not literally, because there isn't a food department at the mall.

Hester is a "plus size." Luckily, she is just a 1X. So she is the smallest of the plus sizes. If that weren't the case, I wouldn't shop with her at all. She gets a kick out of telling the girls at Lane Bryant that she "needs this in a smaller size." And really, when she is decked out (no real pun intended), she looks pretty. Hester has really nice hair.

It doesn't seem right that Hester and I would be friends. I am on the skinny side, and sometimes I just forget to eat.

Wouldn't you think that we just would *not* have one thing in common? But there is more to Hester (geez, another unintended pun) than her size. She is about the most wonderfully generous person in the world. For instance, when she heard about the woman whose husband beat her up and broke her arm, Hester offered to go over there and break *his* arm. It's a good thing Hester's husband and I talked her out of it, because she would have made mincemeat (not again—what's with the puns?) out of him.

Yes, Hester is married. Her husband is Bruce Packmore. He works at a delicatessen, and believe me, what Hester is to desserts, Bruce is to sandwiches. One bite of his pastrami with chopped liver, and you would think you had died and gone to heaven. Bruce is not exactly fat. I would use the adjective "chunky" to describe him. Hester and Bruce are very happily married. But now that Hester is facing fatty liver all by herself, Bruce is losing his patience. She makes things with Splenda now. And she uses that mayonnaise with canola oil. Bruce asked her "Just how much can one man take?" And Hester said, "If I can take it, you can, you big slug!" So things are a little rough over at the Packmores at the moment.

Hester has her weigh-in tomorrow at the doctor's. She bought special lightweight underwear, because she is hoping it will make a difference. She looks a little bit bonier to me, so I am hoping things go well.

Because tomorrow is my birthday, and Bruce and I are certainly going to want more than just a dab of buttercream.

Molly D. Campbell

Characters In Search of a Novel

Horton Gooie

He wears tweeds and smokes a pipe. He likes to tell people that he went to Oxford. Unfortunately for him, he is referring to Oxford, Ohio, where he graduated from Miami University. But he conveniently leaves that part out. And if you call him "Mr. Goo-ey," he will correct you as to the pronunciation: "It's GOOIE—*rhymes with GOY.*"

So Horton is a little bit of a snob. Self-made all the way. Behind the elbow patches is a boy from Shrillwhistle, Tennessee. Yep. Horton grew up on a farm. His father, Melvin Gooie (he pronounced it gooey, and so did everybody else in Shrillwhistle), was a sunburned, taciturn and hard-working man. Not given to saying much. Horty (yep, that's what they called him) was the apple of his mother's eye. Hilda Gooie raised three sons, and Horty was the youngest. Hilda didn't have much time to spare for her children. But what time she did have, she spent telling them stories and reading to them from the one book that she owned (I bet you think it is *The Bible*—wrong): *Webster's Dictionary*. She found it in a Dumpster one time when she was in town. It had a red cover, and it was kind of sticking out. It caught her attention, and when she saw what it was, she grabbed it.

So Horty grew up learning the meaning of words. He and Hilda tried using them in sentences: "There was quite an *imbroglio* at the Dollar Store last Thursday, when Emma Flester tried to steal some batteries," or, "You have a pimple in the upper left *quadrant* of your forehead."

Hilda had high hopes for Horty. And all of this at-home study served him in good stead. That, and the fact that he did very well in school. His teachers all gave him outstanding evaluations, and he did very well on standardized tests. So it was no surprise to anybody when Horty declined a career on the farm in order to go to Oxford. (you know, in Ohio). He got a big scholarship, and what that didn't cover, Hildy made up with the money from the coffee can on the back of the pantry shelf.

So he went to college, majored in Literature, began calling himself *GOY,* and got a job teaching English at Spillwhistle High School. He says he came back home to look after Hilda after Melvin died. Hilda didn't really care for Horton's (he didn't allow "Horty" any more) affectations, but she put up with them. After all, he was her favorite son, and he came home. The other two lived hundreds of miles away.

So Horton Gooie, pronounced GOY, is soon to retire from teaching. When asked what he plans to do in his retirement years, he puffs thoughtfully on his pipe and says "I don't know." But he has an inkling.

I think that there is going to be an *imbroglio* when Hilda discovers that Horton has very little interest in remaining in Spillwhistle forever. I have heard it on the grapevine that Horton wants to move to Columbus, where there is much more cultural activity, and he aims to take Hilda with him. Hilda will have to get rid of the farm, the chickens, and Merle the goat. I have a word for what will probably happen: it will be a *debacle.* Look it up.

Characters In Search of a Novel

Seth Jacobs

His two daughters never understood him. His wife thought he was the strong, silent type. Seth Jacobs kept his thoughts to himself. It wasn't that he had nothing to say: just the contrary. When the horns honked outside his door, Seth imagined just where those people might be going. Sometimes he made up little stories about them in his head. If he saw someone walking down the sidewalk alone, Seth projected that person into a destination, completing it with details like a name and a family.

When Seth was in the third grade, he wrote a story that he was proud of. It was about a boy who knew how to fly. He flew into the air at night, and he looked into people's windows. For some reason, his teacher thought this was worrisome, and she told Seth's mother. His mother, mortified, told Seth that if he *ever* wrote any more stories, she would take him to a doctor. She said it in such a way that Seth realized that there was something wrong with people like him.

As he grew, he continued to make up stories. But he knew better than to share them. With his spending money, he bought notebooks and filled them with imaginings about mysterious deaths, traveling the world, and beautiful things such as blackbirds and mirrors. He wrote stories about curious children and stories about disappointment.

Seth became a worker, a father, and a husband. He made money, took care of his daughters, and kept the yard tidy. His wife tried to engage him in conversation when he got a faraway look, but Seth came right back down to earth and took up the paper or got busy. So things went. Seth kept everything inside his head or in his notebooks. He kept the notebooks secret.

I have never met Seth. But I have read his notebooks. My mother gave them to me for my eighteenth birthday. She told me that my father was really a poet at heart, and that although he was misunderstood by just about everybody, he did reveal himself to her. He was the love of her life, and my mother devoted herself to trying to make my father realize his gifts. She told me about his dreams and his imaginary life. She knew them, because her adoration gave him the confidence to reveal his truths. To her, he was an artist. A few weeks before his death, he gave the notebooks to my mother. He wanted her to have them, because he knew that his wife and daughters would not understand or appreciate them. I will pass them on to my children.

My mother never married. She was Seth Piper's secretary for thirty- two years. I am his only son.

ACANTHA MALWARING

"I think she's a witch. No, I am *sure* of it."

"Oh, me, too. She puts men under her spell, and then they do whatever she wants them to. I bet she has wrecked ten marriages."

"It's her eyes that scare me. I have never seen anyone with such green eyes. I wonder if she wears contact lenses."

"It doesn't make any difference if they're contacts! It's what she *does* with her eyes that is so weird. One time she looked at me from across the *street*, and I suddenly felt all cold and clammy. I had to run into a store to get away from that *look*.

"I heard that when she was five years old, her Mama tried to punish her by putting her in a room all alone, and Acantha just disappeared: poof! And her Mama couldn't find her for hours. Then Acantha just ran in the front door, with a terrible *sneer*. Her Mama has been afraid to cross her ever since."

"Yes, and that's why Acantha is so wild and free. She hasn't had any supervision or rules, because she has always frightened her Mama, and her Daddy just worships the ground she walks on."

"I hear that Dr. Malwaring started taking Acantha to work with him from the time she could walk. She has been around all kinds of chemicals and beakers and things her whole life. I know she performs experiments in her Daddy's laboratory. For all we know, they work together doing horrible things."

"This sounds like Frankenstein!"

"Well you know the story. Acantha fell in love with Richard Fleming when they were in college. He seemed to be completely under her spell, and they were madly in love. Then Richard went away one summer. When he came back, he had met someone else. He tried to break things off. Acantha went wild with fury, and she followed Richard everywhere. She called him and wrote him letters. She stood outside his house. He tried reasoning with her, and he tried avoiding her. He tried to tell people that she was going to hurt him. The police said there was nothing they could do unless she threatened him publicly. But she was relentless. One night at a bar, she went too far, and he hit her. He was dead the next week. Poisoned."

"But no one could prove it was Acantha."

"I know. I know. But there is someone who *can.*"

Characters In Search of a Novel

Persis and Rex

She almost always has the windows open in summer. Air conditioning is a modern horror to her. She likes to sit in shady window when it's hot, and a sunny window when it's cool. She has finch feeders near most of them, and hummingbird feeders near the others. She feeds cardinals on the ground outsider her back door, on a small platform with a bottom made with window screen, for ventilation.

Persis also loves her small house. It's a bungalow, really, but it feels like a cottage to Persis. The Charlesworths moved there when they were early on in their marriage, and Persis herded around two little Charlesworths in the garden, and ran up and down the avenue with them on chilly days after school, when she thought Dennis and little Elise needed just a little more exercise to tire them out before supper.

Persis was "cursed" with bright red hair and freckles. Of course, her husband Rex thought they were captivating. He also admired his wife's small waist and iron determination. For controlling Dennis' foot stamping and Elise's whining seemed something that even a drill sergeant in the Army might wilt under.

Rex and Persis spent time improving their home, making friends with their neighbors, and doing as all the parents in their generation did: they threw baseballs, made picnics, accompanied throngs of seven year olds on field trips to museums which the children found boring and the chaperones fascinating. There were scouting trips, bonfires with cheers, science fairs, and proms.

Suddenly, it seemed like Dennis and Elise were living with their spouses in places thousands of miles away. Elise and her James were stationed in Norway. Dennis was doing a residency in a hospital in New York City.

But Persis and Rex were not blubberers. They waved goodbye, went in the house, straightened their shoulders, and developed new things to keep them busy. Persis took up throwing pots, with often comical results. Rex began painting. And Persis was not afraid to pose in the nude: "Heavens, he sees me in the bathroom every morning; why not just sit down, put lotion on my feet, and read the paper? I did say to Rex that I won't pose when it's drafty. I think October might be a good time to pose in chenille."

Tonight, the Charlesworths had dinner on the brick patio. In early May, there are no pesky bugs to taunt Persis, and Rex can look for hummingbirds through the binoculars. They like to hear the children splashing and screaming at the pool party next door at the McMane's house. They particularly like to listen to the barking of the neighbors' dogs. They sound melodious: some high yips, answered a few houses away by a low, growly "ruff." And then the poodles two doors down bark gaily about the new ball they just got today. The Charlesworths' lovely, old dog Roper died a few weeks ago.

The Charlesworths feel that the living pulse of a neighborhood is its residents. They love diversity. They love children, teens, and newborn babies. They love swimming pools and flower beds. They love conversing with neighbors who are harried parents, and those who are proud grandparents. The Charlesworths have lived in their bungalow in this neighborhood full of interesting and beautiful people for a long time.

At night, they sit on the screened porch and keep track of how many different dogs they hear barking. It's a wonderful way to pass the time in a vibrant and diverse neighborhood. Rex and Elise are in fine fettle and good health. They go up and down their stairs for exercise thirty times a day. Some nights on the screened porch they smooch a little.

Rex is 87, and Elise is 80. They have no plans to move. And what's more, they are puzzled when anyone brings up the subject.

More Characters, Still Searching

Farley Hurlburt: He juggles chickens.

Del Lummish: He loves liver and onions.

Basil Whorls-Feathering: He taught his parrot to swear in Old English.

Fred Stubbs: He has chronic ingrown toenails.

Fanny Fingers: She has sketchy table manners.

Charles Blessings: He has never said the "F" word.

Jon Fxkllysikzy: He wins *tons* of spelling bees.

Andrew Zephyr: He writes terrible poetry but has a lovely voice.

Minerva Pickles: She is a spinster dogsbody extraordinaire.

Tommy Fissbinder: He has no idea what "man up" means.

Stanley Herkimer: He calls his mother twice a day.

Adena Franangelo: She has a very loud voice and big feet.

Joseph Florindo: He sings opera in the garden.

Izzy Stonedrop: She paints her toenails green.

Lucy Crystals: She's bold, bright, and boisterous.

Marvis Bertram: She puts croutons in the bird feeder.

Vlad Jenkins: He thinks he might be a vampire.

Marty Fleff: He always forgets the punch line.

Angela Duffel: She has a lot of emotional baggage.

Plumeria Winkle: She has a rather ample bottom.

Cranston Hasp: His forebears landed at Plymouth Rock.

Alton Lumpley: He thinks fruitcake is delicious.

Hessie Coochers: She's a loose woman, plain and simple.

Denton Plotz: He is baffled by his iPad.

Red Hardacre: He is a violent man.

Afton Ridley: She's a nester.

Dixie Darntoggle: She loves saddle shoes.

Penelope Anacryst: She still uses "gay" to describe happy people.

Darnell Fleckman: Wears wife beaters, but is afraid of his spouse.

Brad Bullfarver: He wears his jock strap to the office.

Seraphina Flutsworth: She is allergic to water.

Verbena Wellesley: She writes couplets while baking meringues.

Whimsey Foss: She's adorable, and everybody loves her.

Tangerine Clevenger: She's a snotty kid.

Cranston Halftwin: He drives a Bentley.

About the Author

Characters In Search of a Novel

Annabricks

My parents named me Molly. I never liked that name. People always wanted to know if my real name was "Margaret." How on earth anybody ever shortened Margaret to Molly was a mystery to me. Plus, my name wasn't Margaret in the first place.

My parents were creative people. Oddballs, I guess. Musicians. So I was an oddball, too. I loved cats, hated school, and most of the time I either worshipped or despised my sister.

There seemed to be a lot of books around. So I read them. I loved *Anne of Green Gables* and Jo March. I knew who Rabelais was by the time I was ten. I used phrases like "the slough of despond" and "pinnacles of ecstasy." And yet, I played with Barbie dolls.

By the time I was in sixth grade, I was the tallest pupil in the entire school, including the principal. Who was a man. Is it any wonder that I wanted to have an alter ego?

So when at home, in the privacy of my room, I became Annabricks. Looking back, I have no idea where the name came from—perhaps a passing infatuation with Butter Brickle ice cream? But as Annabricks, I was chic, famous, worldly, and I ate potato chips with an uplifted pinky. My preferred drink was a Manhattan. Of course, *my* Manhattans were distinctly non-alcoholic and probably consisted of Kool-Aid with a cherry.

Annabricks lived in a penthouse apartment with a terrace. It had high walls around it, so the three Siamese cats (aptly named Maurice, Bunforth, and Marty) could walk around out there without falling off the roof. Annabricks had fascinating friends, and her parents lived next door (I invented Annabricks before I reached puberty—so I needed security).

Annabricks was a saving grace. She got me through the "awkward stage," cat glasses with silver glitter, saddle shoes with knee socks, and biting my nails. She had my back.

If she could grant an interview, Annabricks would most likely have tales to tell of jilted lovers, trips on the backs of camels and elephants, diamond rings the size of golf balls, and crimes of passion. I guess it was Annabricks who invented all of these characters searching for just the right novel to live in. For a while, just after diapers entered my life, Annabricks disappeared. I soldiered on without her, working as a teacher, corporate trainer, and veterinary receptionist—but not all at the same time.

Luckily for me, she showed up again right after my children left home. She started coming up with funny names for people, and then I would try to figure out what those people might be like. So we started on Twitter, and then our partnership grew into a web site, and now, a book! So I raise my glass to Annabricks, who invented all these characters in search. Cheers to her. And may our partnership be long and prosperous.

Molly is a two-time Erma Bombeck Award Winning writer. Follow her on Twitter @mollydcampbell. Her personal blog is http://mollydcampbell.com. A regular writer for the popular Moms' website http://www.momswhoneedwine.com, Molly **is married and the proud mother of two grown**

daughters who pay their own bills. (This is wonderful.)

Molly's husband plays the accordion. (This is tragic.)

Enthusiastic Reviews

"These micro stories tickle the imagination more than a day of people watching at Walmart. Molly Campbell grabs snippets of true 'characters' and spins them into hilarious and oftentimes poignant portraits."

    Beth Hoffman, *New York Times* bestselling Author of *Saving CeeCee Honeycutt*

"A wonderful, original book. Characters in Search of a Novel is richly written with affection and insight for the many unique characters that inhabit the mind of Molly Campbell. In fact, each character is a story; many will make you laugh and a few will break your heart. Sit down and visit with them. You won't regret it."

    Matthew Bombeck

"Wonderfully creative! Molly Campbell's *Characters in Search of a Novel* will make you hope these characters find homes. This book is filled with outrageous characters you'll swear you've met before."

    Tim Bete, Former Director, The Erma Bombeck Writers' Workshop
    Author of *Guide to Pirate Parenting.*

"Molly has a love of language and a way with words that is just infectious. Combine that with a perspective on life that is both small-town and enormously worldly (however that's possible)—and you've got the recipe for some outstanding storytelling. In *Characters in Search of a Novel,* Molly gives us a series of snippets that are—under the guise of character biographies—brilliant little stories of fiction in themselves. They make us laugh, cry and, well, want to hug (even the weirdest ones). Reading her novel is like sitting on a park bench and watching the world go by. One lovely, intriguing character at a time."

Marile Borden, Founder & Editor, **www.MomsWhoNeedWine.com**

Made in the USA
Charleston, SC
21 September 2012